Keto Air Fryer Cookbook for Beginners

Delicious Low Carb Recipes for Quick Weight Loss | 28-Day Meal Plan with Easy Ketogenic Ideas to Support a Healthy Lifestyle and Sustainable Eating

TATTI WOLF

Table of Contents

Introduction
What is the Keto Diet?

Alright, let's talk about the Keto Diet! You've probably heard all the buzz about it by now—it's that high-fat, low-carb way of eating that everyone seems to be trying. The idea behind keto is pretty simple: you cut back on carbs big time and load up on fats. This switch convinces your body to start using fat as its main energy source instead of sugar. When this happens, you enter a state called ketosis, where your liver turns fat into ketones, and boom! Your body becomes a fat-burning machine.

The basic breakdown of the Keto Diet is about 70-75% of your daily calories coming from fats, 15-20% from protein, and only about 5-10% from carbs. So think creamy avocados, olive oil, buttery goodness, and fatty fish as your new best friends, while saying goodbye to sugar, bread, and potatoes.

Benefits of the Keto Diet

So why do people get so hyped about keto? Well, one of the biggest reasons is its superpower when it comes to weight loss. Since your body is burning fat for fuel, a lot of folks see the pounds drop off, especially when they pair it with mindful eating. But it's not just about shedding weight—going keto can help stabilize your blood sugar, which is a huge win if you've got type 2 diabetes.

Plus, keto isn't just a diet; it can be a whole lifestyle upgrade. It's been linked to lower inflammation, better mental clarity (goodbye, brain fog!), and even improvements in heart health by boosting those "good" HDL cholesterol levels. And there's more—some studies suggest keto might even help you live longer by reducing oxidative stress and protecting your brain.

And let's be real, who doesn't love the idea of having more energy, fewer cravings, and a sharper focus? That's why so many people rave about how they just feel better on keto—like they've hit their groove.

How the Air Fryer Works for Keto Cooking

If you're all about keto, then you're going to love what the air fryer brings to the table. This kitchen gadget is like magic for keto cooks! It uses hot air to make your food crispy and delicious without drowning it in oil. This means you get all that crunchy goodness while sticking to your keto goals—no starchy coatings or heavy breading needed.

Imagine making keto-friendly chicken wings, crispy bacon, or roasted veggies with hardly any oil, all while keeping the flavor and crunch that you crave. The best part? You're in control of the fats you use, so you can make sure they're the healthy kinds that work perfectly with your keto lifestyle.

And let's not forget how fast and easy it is to whip up meals in the air fryer! Less mess, less cleanup, and more time enjoying your food. It's the ultimate tool to make your keto journey smoother and way more delicious.

Essential Tools and Ingredients for Keto Cooking

Now, let's talk gear! When you're going keto, having the right tools in your kitchen can make all the difference. Of course, the air fryer is a must, but there are a few other gadgets that'll make your keto life way easier. A solid blender is great for making creamy smoothies or sauces, and a spiralizer can turn zucchini into noodle magic. And if you haven't already, grab yourself a good cast-iron skillet or a non-stick pan—they're perfect for those protein-packed meals.

On the ingredient front, stocking up on keto essentials will save you from those "what do I eat?" moments. Here's a quick list of must-haves:

- **Healthy fats:** Think coconut oil, olive oil, butter, ghee, and avocado oil.
- **Protein sources:** Grass-fed meats, fatty fish like salmon, free-range eggs, and even plant-based proteins like tofu.
- **Low-carb veggies:** Load up on leafy greens, cauliflower, zucchini, and broccoli.
- **Keto-friendly flours:** Almond flour, coconut flour, and flaxseed meal for all your baking needs.
- **Dairy goodies:** Full-fat cheese, heavy cream, and Greek yogurt to keep things rich and creamy.
- **Nuts and seeds:** Almonds, macadamia nuts, chia seeds, and flaxseeds are awesome for snacking.

With these tools and ingredients, you'll be all set to whip up mouth-watering keto dishes whenever hunger strikes. Whether you're frying up a quick stir-fry, blending a creamy soup, or baking a decadent keto dessert, having the right stuff in your kitchen means you'll always be on track with your keto lifestyle. Let's get cooking!

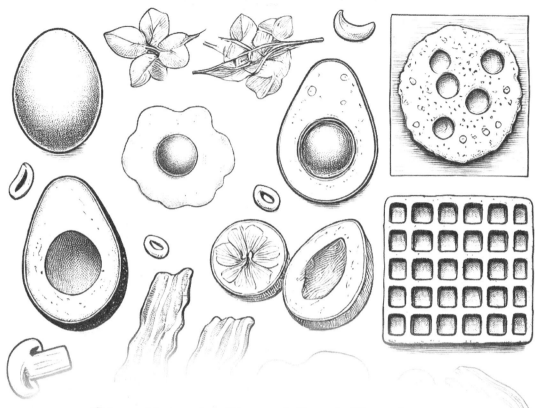

Chapter 1: Breakfast Recipes

Cheesy Egg Bites

Prep Time: 10 min   **Cook Time: 15 min**   **Serves: 2**

INGREDIENTS:

- 6 large eggs
- 1/2 cup heavy cream
- 1/2 cup shredded cheddar cheese (or any keto-friendly cheese, like gouda or mozzarella)
- 1/4 cup cream cheese, softened
- 1/4 cup cooked bacon bits (optional, for extra flavor and protein)
- 1/4 cup chopped spinach or kale (optional, for added fiber)
- 1/4 tsp garlic powder
- 1/4 tsp onion powder
- Salt and pepper to taste
- Cooking spray or a bit of olive oil (to coat the molds)

DIRECTIONS:

1. In a medium bowl, whisk together the eggs, heavy cream, cream cheese, garlic powder, onion powder, salt, and pepper until smooth. **2.** Stir in the shredded cheese, bacon bits, and spinach or kale (if using). **3.** Grease silicone molds or ramekins that fit your air fryer with cooking spray or olive oil. Pour the egg mixture evenly into the molds, filling them about 3/4 of the way. **4.** Preheat the air fryer to 300°F (150°C). Place the molds in the air fryer and cook for 12-15 minutes, or until the egg bites are set and lightly golden on top. Rotate the basket halfway through cooking for even heat distribution. **5.** Once cooked, let the egg bites cool for a couple of minutes before removing them from the molds. Serve warm.

NUTRITIONAL INFORMATION

Per serving: 260 calories, 12g protein, 2g carbohydrates, 22g fat, 0.5g fiber, 210mg cholesterol, 320mg sodium, 150mg potassium.

Bacon and Egg Muffins

Prep Time: 10 min   **Cook Time: 10 min**   **Serves: 6**

INGREDIENTS:

- 6 slices bacon
- 6 large eggs
- 1/4 cup shredded cheddar cheese
- 2 tbsp heavy cream
- 1/2 tsp salt
- 1/4 tsp black pepper
- Optional: chopped spinach or diced bell peppers for added nutrition

DIRECTIONS:

1. Preheat air fryer to 350°F (180°C). **2** Cook bacon slices in the air fryer for 4-5 minutes until slightly crispy. Drain excess fat. **3.** In a bowl, whisk together eggs, heavy cream, salt, and pepper. Stir in cheddar cheese and any optional ingredients. **4.** Line each compartment of a silicone muffin mold with a bacon slice. **5.** Pour the egg mixture evenly into each bacon-lined compartment. **6.** Place the mold in the air fryer and cook at 350°F (180°C) for 8-10 minutes, or until the eggs are set. **7.** Shake the basket midway through cooking to ensure even cooking.

NUTRITIONAL INFORMATION

190 calories, 12g protein, 2g carbohydrates, 15g fat, 0.5g fiber, 170mg cholesterol, 290mg sodium, 120mg potassium.

Sausage and Cheese Omelet

INGREDIENTS:

- 4 large eggs
- 1/4 cup heavy cream
- 1/2 cup shredded cheddar cheese (or cheese of choice)
- 1/2 cup cooked sausage crumbles (breakfast sausage or any keto-friendly sausage)
- 1/4 cup chopped spinach or kale (optional for added nutrients)
- 1 tbsp butter (optional for extra richness)
- Salt and pepper to taste
- Cooking spray or olive oil for greasing
- Silicone molds or ramekins that fit your air fryer

Prep Time: 5 min   **Cook Time: 12 min**   **Serves: 2**

DIRECTIONS:

1. In a medium bowl, whisk together the eggs, heavy cream, salt, and pepper until smooth and well combined. **2.** Stir in the shredded cheese, cooked sausage crumbles, and chopped spinach or kale (if using). **3.** Lightly grease the silicone molds or ramekins with cooking spray or olive oil. **4.** Evenly divide the egg mixture between the molds, filling each about 3/4 full. **5.** Preheat the air fryer to 330°F (165°C). **6.** Place the filled molds in the air fryer basket, ensuring they are not overcrowded for even heat circulation. **7.** Cook for 10-12 minutes, or until the omelet is fully set and golden on top. Rotate the basket halfway through cooking to ensure even heat distribution. **8.** Once cooked, allow the omelet to cool for a minute before carefully removing it from the molds. Serve warm.

NUTRITIONAL INFORMATION

Per serving: 390 calories, 22g protein, 3g carbohydrates, 33g fat, 0.5g fiber, 295mg cholesterol, 620mg sodium, 210mg potassium.

Pancakes with Almond Flour

INGREDIENTS:

- 1 cup almond flour
- 2 large eggs
- 1/4 cup unsweetened almond milk (or heavy cream for a richer taste)
- 2 tbsp melted butter (plus more for greasing)
- 1 tsp vanilla extract
- 1/2 tsp baking powder
- 1/4 tsp cinnamon (optional for flavor)
- 1-2 tbsp erythritol or other keto-friendly sweetener (optional)
- Pinch of salt

мPrep Time: 5 min   **Cook Time: 10 min**   **Serves: 2**

DIRECTIONS:

1. In a bowl, whisk almond flour, baking powder, cinnamon, and salt. **2.** In another bowl, whisk eggs, almond milk, butter, vanilla, and sweetener. **3.** Combine the wet and dry ingredients, stirring until smooth. Let the batter sit for a few minutes to thicken. **4.** Grease silicone molds or an air fryer-safe pan with butter or spray. **5.** Pour the batter into molds or the pan, spreading it evenly. **6.** Preheat air fryer to 320°F (160°C). **7.** Cook for 8-10 minutes, flipping halfway through, until golden brown. **8.** Remove pancakes from air fryer, let cool slightly, and serve..

NUTRITIONAL INFORMATION

Per serving (2 pancakes): 270 calories, 10g protein, 5g carbohydrates, 24g fat, 3g fiber, 140mg cholesterol, 190mg sodium, 180mg potassium.

Avocado and Bacon Egg Cups

INGREDIENTS:
- 2 ripe avocados
- 4 large eggs
- 4 slices cooked bacon, crumbled
- Salt and pepper to taste
- 1/4 tsp garlic powder (optional)
- 1/4 tsp smoked paprika (optional for flavor)
- Cooking spray or olive oil

Prep Time: 5 min **Cook Time: 15 min** **Serves: 4**

DIRECTIONS:
1. Cut avocados in half and remove the pits. Scoop out some flesh to create space for the eggs. **2.** Season each avocado half with salt, pepper, garlic powder, and paprika. **3.** Crack an egg into each avocado half, being careful not to overflow. **4.** Top with crumbled bacon. **5.** Preheat the air fryer to 350°F (175°C). **6.** Place the avocado halves in the air fryer basket and cook for 12-15 minutes, or until the eggs are set. **7.** Rotate the basket halfway through for even cooking. **8.** Once done, remove and let cool for a minute before serving.

NUTRITIONAL INFORMATION
Per serving: 320 calories, 10g protein, 8g carbohydrates, 28g fat, 6g fiber, 220mg cholesterol, 300mg sodium, 480mg potassium.

Coconut Flour Waffles

INGREDIENTS:
- 1/4 cup coconut flour
- 3 large eggs
- 2 tbsp melted butter or coconut oil
- 1/4 cup unsweetened almond milk
- 1 tsp vanilla extract
- 1/2 tsp baking powder
- 1 tbsp erythritol or other keto-friendly sweetener (optional)
- Pinch of salt

Prep Time: 5 min **Cook Time: 10 min** **Serves: 2**

DIRECTIONS:
1. In a bowl, whisk eggs, melted butter, almond milk, and vanilla extract. **2.** Add coconut flour, baking powder, sweetener, and salt. Stir until smooth and let sit for 2 minutes to thicken. **3.** Lightly grease silicone waffle molds or an air fryer-safe pan with cooking spray. **4.** Pour batter evenly into molds, spreading it out. **5.** Preheat air fryer to 320°F (160°C). **7.** Cook waffles for 8-10 minutes until golden. Rotate the basket halfway through for even cooking. **8.** Once done, carefully remove waffles and let cool slightly.

NUTRITIONAL INFORMATION
Per serving (2 waffles): 220 calories, 9g protein, 6g carbohydrates, 18g fat, 4g fiber, 170mg cholesterol, 200mg sodium, 160mg potassium.

Spinach and Feta Breakfast Frittata

INGREDIENTS:
- 4 large eggs
- 6 large eggs
- 1/4 cup heavy cream
- 1/2 cup crumbled feta cheese
- 1 cup fresh spinach, chopped
- 1/4 cup diced onions (optional)
- 1 tbsp olive oil or melted butter
- Salt and pepper to taste
- 1/4 tsp garlic powder (optional)

Prep Time: 5 min   **Cook Time: 15 min**   **Serves: 4**

DirEctions:
1. In a bowl, whisk eggs, heavy cream, salt, pepper, and garlic powder (if using). **2.** Stir in chopped spinach, onions, and crumbled feta cheese. **3.** Grease an air fryer-safe dish with olive oil or butter. **4.** Pour the egg mixture into the dish, spreading it evenly. **5.** Preheat the air fryer to 350°F (175°C). **6.** Cook the frittata for 12-15 minutes until the eggs are fully set. Rotate the dish halfway through cooking to ensure even heat distribution. **7.** Once done, remove from the air fryer and let cool for a minute before slicing.

NUTRITIONAL INFORMATION
Per serving: 280 calories, 14g protein, 4g carbohydrates, 24g fat, 1g fiber, 260mg cholesterol, 320mg sodium, 210mg potassium.

Ham and Cheese Egg Rolls

INGREDIENTS:
- 6 slices of deli ham
- 3 large eggs
- 1/2 cup shredded cheddar or Swiss cheese
- 1 tbsp heavy cream
- 1 tbsp butter
- Salt and pepper to taste
- 1/4 tsp garlic powder (optional)
- Cooking spray or olive oil

Prep Time: 5 min   **Cook Time: 10 min**   **Serves: 3**

DIRECTIONS:
1. In a bowl, whisk the eggs, heavy cream, salt, pepper, and garlic powder. **2.** Heat butter in a skillet and scramble the eggs until just set. Let them cool slightly. **3.** Lay out ham slices, evenly divide scrambled eggs and cheese across each slice. **4.** Roll up the ham slices tightly and secure with toothpicks if needed. **5.** Preheat the air fryer to 350°F (175°C). **6.** Lightly grease the air fryer basket with cooking spray and place the ham rolls seam side down. **7.** Cook for 8-10 minutes until the rolls are golden and cheese is melted, flipping halfway through.

NUTRITIONAL INFORMATION
Per serving: 290 calories, 20g protein, 2g carbohydrates, 23g fat, 0g fiber, 210mg cholesterol, 670mg sodium, 150mg potassium.

Cinnamon French Toast Sticks

Prep Time: 5 min   **Cook Time: 10 min**   **Serves: 2**

INGREDIENTS:

* 4 slices of keto-friendly bread
* 2 large eggs
* 1/4 cup heavy cream
* 1 tsp cinnamon
* 1 tbsp erythritol or other keto-friendly sweetener
* 1 tsp vanilla extract
* 1 tbsp melted butter
* Cooking spray or olive oil

DIRECTIONS:

1. Cut the keto bread slices into 3 sticks per slice. **2.** In a bowl, whisk eggs, heavy cream, cinnamon, sweetener, and vanilla. **3.** Dip each bread stick into the mixture, ensuring it's fully coated. **4.** Preheat the air fryer to 350°F (175°C). **5.** Lightly grease the air fryer basket with cooking spray. **6.** Place the dipped bread sticks in the basket, making sure they don't overlap. **7.** Cook for 8-10 minutes, flipping halfway through until golden and crispy. **8.** Brush the finished sticks with melted butter..

NUTRITIONAL INFORMATION

Per serving: 280 calories, 10g protein, 4g carbohydrates, 24g fat, 2g fiber, 215mg cholesterol, 250mg sodium, 160mg potassium.

Breakfast Sausage Patties

Prep Time: 5 min   **Cook Time: 10 min**   **Serves: 4**

INGREDIENTS:

* 1 lb ground pork
* 1 tsp garlic powder
* 1 tsp onion powder
* 1/2 tsp paprika
* 1/2 tsp dried thyme
* 1/2 tsp ground sage
* 1/4 tsp crushed red pepper flakes (optional)
* Salt and pepper to taste
* Cooking spray or olive oil

DIRECTIONS:

1. In a bowl, combine ground pork, garlic powder, onion powder, paprika, thyme, sage, red pepper flakes, salt, and pepper. Mix well. **2.** Form the mixture into 8 small patties. **3.** Preheat the air fryer to 370°F (185°C). **4.** Lightly grease the air fryer basket with cooking spray or oil. **5.** Place the patties in the basket, ensuring they do not overlap. **6.** Cook for 8-10 minutes, flipping halfway through until fully cooked and golden. **7.** Ensure the internal temperature reaches 160°F (70°C) for safety.

NUTRITIONAL INFORMATION

Per serving: 300 calories, 20g protein, 1g carbohydrates, 24g fat, 0g fiber, 80mg cholesterol, 400mg sodium, 350mg potassium.

Zucchini and Egg Breakfast Casserole

INGREDIENTS:
- 1 medium zucchini, grated and drained
- 6 large eggs
- 1/2 cup shredded cheddar cheese
- 1/4 cup heavy cream
- 1/4 cup diced onions (optional)
- 1/4 tsp garlic powder
- 1/4 tsp paprika
- Salt and pepper to taste
- Cooking spray or olive oil

Prep Time: 10 min   **Cook Time: 15 min**   **Serves: 4**

DIRECTIONS:
1. Grate the zucchini, squeeze out excess moisture, and set aside. **2.** In a bowl, whisk eggs, heavy cream, garlic powder, paprika, salt, and pepper. **3.** Stir in grated zucchini, cheese, and onions (if using). **4.** Lightly grease an air fryer-safe dish with cooking spray or oil. **5.** Pour the mixture into the dish, spreading it evenly. **6.** Preheat the air fryer to 350°F (175°C). **7.** Cook for 12-15 minutes until the eggs are set and golden on top. Rotate the dish halfway through for even cooking. **8.** Let cool slightly before serving.

NUTRITIONAL INFORMATION
Per serving: 220 calories, 14g protein, 5g carbohydrates, 17g fat, 1g fiber, 250mg cholesterol, 320mg sodium, 260mg potassium.

Keto Chaffles (Cheese Waffles)

INGREDIENTS:
- 1 cup shredded mozzarella or cheddar cheese
- 2 large eggs
- 2 tbsp almond flour (optional for added texture)
- 1/2 tsp baking powder
- 1/4 tsp garlic powder (optional)
- Salt and pepper to taste
- Cooking spray or olive oil

Prep Time: 5 min   **Cook Time: 10 min**   **Serves: 2**

DIRECTIONS:
1. In a bowl, whisk eggs, then add cheese, almond flour, baking powder, garlic powder, salt, and pepper. Mix well. **2.** Lightly grease silicone waffle molds or an air fryer-safe pan with cooking spray. **3.** Pour the chaffle batter into the molds, spreading evenly. **4.** Preheat the air fryer to 350°F (175°C). **5.** Cook for 8-10 minutes until the chaffles are golden and crisp. Flip or rotate the basket halfway through for even cooking. **6.** Once done, let the chaffles cool slightly before serving.

NUTRITIONAL INFORMATION
Per serving (2 chaffles): 280 calories, 20g protein, 3g carbohydrates, 22g fat, 1g fiber, 230mg cholesterol, 400mg sodium, 180mg potassium.

Keto Breakfast Burrito

INGREDIENTS:

- 4 large eggs
- 1/2 cup cooked sausage or bacon, crumbled
- 1/2 cup shredded cheddar cheese
- 1/4 cup diced bell peppers (optional)
- 1/4 cup diced onions (optional)
- 2 large keto tortillas
- 1 tbsp butter or olive oil
- Salt and pepper to taste

Prep Time: 5 min   **Cook Time: 10 min**   **Serves: 2**

DIRECTIONS:

1. In a pan, scramble eggs with butter until just set. Season with salt and pepper. **2.** Lay the keto tortillas flat, evenly distribute the scrambled eggs, sausage, cheese, and optional peppers and onions. **3.** Roll the tortillas into burritos, tucking the sides in. **4.** Preheat the air fryer to 350°F (175°C). **5.** Place the burritos seam-side down in the air fryer basket. Cook for 8-10 minutes, flipping halfway through, until the burritos are golden and crisp. **6.** Let the burritos cool slightly before serving.

NUTRITIONAL INFORMATION

Per serving (1 burrito): 400 calories, 22g protein, 6g carbohydrates, 32g fat, 2g fiber, 310mg cholesterol, 580mg sodium, 210mg potassium.

Cauliflower Hash Browns

INGREDIENTS:

- 2 cups cauliflower rice (fresh or frozen, drained)
- 1 large egg
- 1/2 cup shredded cheddar cheese
- 1/4 cup almond flour
- 1/2 tsp garlic powder
- 1/2 tsp onion powder
- Salt and pepper to taste
- Cooking spray or olive oil

Prep Time: 10 min   **мCook Time: 12 min**   **Serves: 4**

DIRECTIONS:

1. In a bowl, combine cauliflower rice, egg, cheese, almond flour, garlic powder, onion powder, salt, and pepper. Mix well. **2.** Form small patties from the mixture and place them on parchment paper. **3.** Preheat the air fryer to 375°F (190°C). **4.** Lightly grease the air fryer basket with cooking spray or olive oil. **5.** Place patties in the basket, ensuring they do not overlap. **6.** Cook for 10-12 minutes, flipping halfway through, until golden and crispy. **7.** Remove and let cool slightly before serving.

NUTRITIONAL INFORMATION

Per serving: 130 calories, 8g protein, 4g carbohydrates, 9g fat, 2g fiber, 60mg cholesterol, 200mg sodium, 150mg potassium.

Keto Scotch Eggs

INGREDIENTS:

- 4 large eggs (soft or hard-boiled)
- 1 lb ground sausage (pork or beef)
- 1/2 cup almond flour
- 1 tsp garlic powder
- 1 tsp onion powder
- 1/2 tsp paprika
- Salt and pepper to taste
- Cooking spray or olive oil

Prep Time: 10 min   **Cook Time: 15 min**   **Serves: 4**

DIRECTIONS:

1. Peel the boiled eggs and set aside. **2.** Season the ground sausage with garlic powder, onion powder, paprika, salt, and pepper. **3.** Divide the sausage into 4 portions. Flatten each portion and wrap it around each egg, fully covering it. **4.** Roll each wrapped egg in almond flour to coat. **5.** Preheat the air fryer to 375°F (190°C). **6.** Lightly grease the air fryer basket with cooking spray. **7.** Place the scotch eggs in the basket, ensuring they don't touch. Cook for 12-15 minutes, flipping halfway, until golden brown. **8.** Let cool slightly before serving.

NUTRITIONAL INFORMATION

Per serving: 350 calories, 20g protein, 3g carbohydrates, 28g fat, 1g fiber, 230mg cholesterol, 600mg sodium, 280mg potassium.

Mushroom and Bacon Breakfast Bake

INGREDIENTS:

- 6 large eggs
- 1/2 cup heavy cream
- 1 cup sliced mushrooms
- 1/2 cup cooked bacon, crumbled
- 1/2 cup shredded cheddar cheese
- 1/4 tsp garlic powder
- 1/4 tsp onion powder
- Salt and pepper to taste
- Cooking spray or olive oil

Prep Time: 10 min   **Cook Time: 15 min**   **мServes: 4**

DIRECTIONS:

1. In a bowl, whisk eggs, heavy cream, garlic powder, onion powder, salt, and pepper. **2.** Stir in mushrooms, bacon, and shredded cheese. **3.** Grease an air fryer-safe dish with cooking spray or oil. **4.** Pour the egg mixture into the dish, spreading evenly. **5.** Preheat the air fryer to 350°F (175°C). **6.** Cook for 12-15 minutes, until the eggs are fully set and the top is golden brown. Rotate the dish halfway through cooking for even heat distribution. **7.** Let cool slightly before serving.

NUTRITIONAL INFORMATION

Per serving: 320 calories, 18g protein, 4g carbohydrates, 26g fat, 1g fiber, 250mg cholesterol, 450mg sodium, 280mg potassium.

Keto Egg Muffins with Veggies

INGREDIENTS:

- 6 large eggs
- 1/4 cup heavy cream
- 1/2 cup chopped spinach
- 1/4 cup diced bell peppers
- 1/4 cup shredded cheddar cheese
- 1/4 tsp salt
- 1/4 tsp black pepper
- Optional: 2 tbsp chopped mushrooms or diced onions

Prep Time: 10 min   **Cook Time: 10 min**   **Serves: 6 muffins**

DIRECTIONS:

1. Preheat the air fryer to 350°F (180°C). **2.** In a bowl, whisk eggs, heavy cream, salt, and pepper until well combined. **3.** Stir in spinach, bell peppers, cheese, and any optional ingredients. **4.** Divide the mixture evenly into a silicone muffin mold. **5.** Place the mold in the air fryer and cook at 350°F (180°C) for 8-10 minutes, or until the eggs are set. **6.** Shake the basket midway through cooking for even heat distribution. **7.** Serving Suggestion: Enjoy warm for breakfast or as a high-protein snack.

NUTRITIONAL INFORMATION

120 calories, 8g protein, 2g carbohydrates, 9g fat, 0.5g fiber, 150mg cholesterol, 180mg sodium, 100mg potassium.

Chorizo and Cheese Breakfast Skillet

INGREDIENTS:

- 200g chorizo sausage, diced
- 4 large eggs
- 1/2 cup shredded cheddar cheese
- 1/4 cup diced bell peppers
- 1/4 cup chopped onions
- 1/4 tsp salt
- 1/4 tsp black pepper
- Optional: 2 tbsp chopped spinach or diced tomatoes

Prep Time: 5 min   **Cook Time: 12 min**   **Serves: 2**

DIRECTIONS:

1. Preheat the air fryer to 350°F (180°C). **2.** Cook chorizo in the air fryer basket for 5 minutes, shaking halfway. **3.** In a bowl, whisk eggs, salt, and pepper. **4.** Add bell peppers, onions, and optional ingredients to the egg mixture. **5.** Pour the egg mix over the chorizo and sprinkle with cheese. **6.** Cook in the air fryer at 350°F (180°C) for 7 minutes or until eggs are set. **7.** Shake the basket midway for even cooking. Serving Suggestion: Serve hot with avocado slices.

NUTRITIONAL INFORMATION

340 calories, 22g protein, 3g carbohydrates, 27g fat, 1g fiber, 210mg cholesterol, 480mg sodium, 250mg potassium.

Almond Flour Crepes

INGREDIENTS:

- 1/2 cup almond flour
- 2 large eggs
- 2 tbsp heavy cream
- 2 tbsp water
- 1/4 tsp vanilla extract
- 1/4 tsp salt
- Optional: 1/4 tsp cinnamon or 1 tsp sweetener

Prep Time: 5 min **мCook Time: 8 min** **Serves: 4 crepes**

DIRECTIONS:

1. Preheat the air fryer to 320°F (160°C). **2.** In a bowl, whisk almond flour, eggs, cream, water, vanilla, salt, and optional ingredients. **3.** Pour a thin layer of the batter into a silicone baking sheet that fits your air fryer. **4.** Cook at 320°F (160°C) for 4 minutes, then flip and cook for an additional 3-4 minutes. **5.** Repeat with the remaining batter. **6.** Tip: For even cooking, ensure the batter is spread thin and even.
Serving Suggestion: Serve warm with sugar-free syrup or berries.

NUTRITIONAL INFORMATION

110 calories, 5g protein, 2g carbohydrates, 9g fat, 1g fiber, 55mg cholesterol, 70mg sodium, 40mg potassium.

Breakfast Casserole with Sausage and Spinach

INGREDIENTS:

- 200g ground sausage
- 4 large eggs
- 1/2 cup chopped spinach
- 1/4 cup shredded mozzarella cheese
- 2 tbsp heavy cream
- 1/4 tsp salt
- 1/4 tsp black pepper
- Optional: 2 tbsp diced bell peppers or mushrooms

Prep Time: 5 min **Cook Time: 15 min** **Serves: 4**

DIRECTIONS:

1. Preheat the air fryer to 350°F (180°C). **2.** Cook sausage in the air fryer basket for 5 minutes. **3.** In a bowl, whisk eggs, cream, salt, and pepper. **4.** Add spinach, cheese, and optional ingredients to the egg mixture. **5.** Pour over the sausage in a baking dish that fits your air fryer. **6.** Cook at 350°F (180°C) for 10 minutes, shaking halfway.
Serving Suggestion: Serve warm with a side of avocado or low-carb toast.

NUTRITIONAL INFORMATION

210 calories, 15g protein, 3g carbohydrates, 16g fat, 1g fiber, 180mg cholesterol, 420mg sodium, 160mg potassium.

Chapter 2: Appetizers and Snacks

Spicy Jalapeño Poppers

INGREDIENTS:

- 8 large jalapeños, halved and seeded
- 4 oz cream cheese, softened
- 1/2 cup shredded cheddar cheese
- 4 slices cooked bacon, crumbled
- 1/2 tsp garlic powder
- 1/4 tsp smoked paprika
- Salt and pepper to taste
- Cooking spray or olive oil

Prep Time: 10 min   **Cook Time: 10 min**   **Serves: 4**

DIRECTIONS:

1. In a bowl, mix cream cheese, cheddar, bacon, garlic powder, smoked paprika, salt, and pepper. **2.** Stuff each jalapeño half with the cream cheese mixture. **3.** Preheat the air fryer to 375°F (190°C). **4.** Lightly grease the air fryer basket with cooking spray or oil. **5.** Place the stuffed jalapeños in the basket, ensuring they do not overlap. **6.** Cook for 8-10 minutes, until the jalapeños are tender and the cheese is bubbly and golden. Shake the basket halfway through for even cooking. **7.** Let cool slightly before serving.

NUTRITIONAL INFORMATION

Per serving: 180 calories, 6g protein, 4g carbohydrates, 15g fat, 1g fiber, 30mg cholesterol, 250mg sodium, 150mg potassium.

Buffalo Chicken Wings

INGREDIENTS:

- 2 lbs chicken wings
- 1/2 tsp garlic powder
- 1/2 tsp onion powder
- 1/2 tsp smoked paprika
- Salt and pepper to taste
- 1/4 cup unsalted butter, melted
- 1/4 cup hot sauce (like Frank's RedHot)
- Cooking spray or olive oil

Prep Time: 5 min   **Cook Time: 25 min**   **Serves: 4**

DIRECTIONS:

1. Pat the chicken wings dry with a paper towel. **2.** In a bowl, mix garlic powder, onion powder, paprika, salt, and pepper. Toss the wings in the spice mix. **3.** Preheat the air fryer to 375°F (190°C). **4.** Lightly grease the air fryer basket with cooking spray or oil. **5.** Place wings in the basket in a single layer and cook for 20-25 minutes, flipping halfway through, until crispy and fully cooked (internal temperature should reach 165°F). **6.** While the wings cook, mix melted butter and hot sauce. **7.** Toss cooked wings in the buffalo sauce mixture.

NUTRITIONAL INFORMATION

Per serving: 350 calories, 25g protein, 2g carbohydrates, 28g fat, 0g fiber, 140mg cholesterol, 800mg sodium, 220mg potassium.

Parmesan Zucchini Chips

INGREDIENTS:
- 2 medium zucchinis, thinly sliced
- 1/2 cup grated Parmesan cheese
- 1/2 tsp garlic powder
- 1/2 tsp paprika
- Salt and pepper to taste
- Cooking spray or olive oil

Prep Time: 5 min   **Cook Time: 12 min**   **Serves: 4**

DIRECTIONS:
1. Thinly slice the zucchinis and pat them dry with a paper towel to remove excess moisture. **2.** In a bowl, mix Parmesan, garlic powder, paprika, salt, and pepper. **3.** Toss zucchini slices in the cheese mixture, ensuring each slice is coated. **4.** Preheat the air fryer to 375°F (190°C). **5.** Lightly grease the air fryer basket with cooking spray or oil. **6.** Place zucchini slices in a single layer in the basket and cook for 10-12 minutes, shaking the basket halfway through, until golden and crispy. **7.** Remove chips and let them cool slightly before serving.

NUTRITIONAL INFORMATION
Per serving: 100 calories, 5g protein, 3g carbohydrates, 7g fat, 1g fiber, 10mg cholesterol, 200mg sodium, 150mg potassium.

Crispy Cauliflower Bites

INGREDIENTS:
- 1 medium head cauliflower, cut into bite-sized florets
- 1/2 cup almond flour
- 1/4 cup grated Parmesan cheese
- 1 tsp garlic powder
- 1/2 tsp paprika
- 1/2 tsp salt
- 1/4 tsp black pepper
- 1 large egg, beaten
- Cooking spray or olive oil

Prep Time: 10 min   **Cook Time: 15 min**   **Serves: 4**

DIRECTIONS:
1. In a bowl, mix almond flour, Parmesan, garlic powder, paprika, salt, and pepper. **2.** Dip each cauliflower floret into the beaten egg, then coat with the almond flour mixture. **3.** Preheat the air fryer to 375°F (190°C). **4.** Lightly grease the air fryer basket with cooking spray or oil. **5.** Place the coated cauliflower in the basket in a single layer. Cook for 12-15 minutes, shaking the basket halfway through, until golden and crispy. **6.** Let the cauliflower cool slightly before serving.

NUTRITIONAL INFORMATION
Per serving: 140 calories, 6g protein, 5g carbohydrates, 10g fat, 3g fiber, 40mg cholesterol, 250mg sodium, 300mg potassium.

Avocado Fries

INGREDIENTS:

- 2 ripe avocados, cut into wedges
- 1/2 cup almond flour
- 1/4 cup grated Parmesan cheese
- 1/2 tsp garlic powder
- 1/2 tsp paprika
- 1/4 tsp salt
- 1/4 tsp black pepper
- 1 large egg, beaten
- Cooking spray or olive oil

Prep Time: 10 min **Cook Time: 10 min** **Serves: 4**

DIRECTIONS:

1. In a bowl, mix almond flour, Parmesan, garlic powder, paprika, salt, and pepper. **2.** Dip each avocado wedge into the beaten egg, then coat with the almond flour mixture. **3.** Preheat the air fryer to 350°F (175°C). **4.** Lightly grease the air fryer basket with cooking spray or oil. **5.** Place avocado wedges in the basket in a single layer. Cook for 8-10 minutes, flipping halfway through, until crispy and golden. **6.** Let the fries cool slightly before serving.

NUTRITIONAL INFORMATION

Per serving: 220 calories, 4g protein, 8g carbohydrates, 19g fat, 6g fiber, 55mg cholesterol, 180mg sodium, 380mg potassium.

Cheesy Stuffed Mushrooms

INGREDIENTS:

- 12 large button mushrooms, stems removed
- 1/2 cup cream cheese, softened
- 1/4 cup shredded mozzarella cheese
- 1/4 cup grated Parmesan cheese
- 2 cloves garlic, minced
- 1 tbsp chopped parsley (optional)
- Salt and pepper to taste
- Cooking spray or olive oil

Prep Time: 10 min **Cook Time: 10 min** **Serves: 4**

DIRECTIONS:

1. Preheat the air fryer to 350°F (175°C). **2.** In a bowl, mix cream cheese, mozzarella, Parmesan, garlic, parsley, salt, and pepper until smooth. **3.** Stuff each mushroom cap with the cheese mixture, filling them generously. **4.** Lightly grease the air fryer basket with cooking spray or oil. **5.** Arrange the stuffed mushrooms in a single layer in the basket. **6.** Cook for 8-10 minutes, until the mushrooms are tender and the cheese is bubbly and golden. Rotate or shake the basket halfway through for even cooking. **7.** Let cool slightly before serving.

NUTRITIONAL INFORMATION

Per serving: 180 calories, 7g protein, 4g carbohydrates, 15g fat, 1g fiber, 40mg cholesterol, 250mg sodium, 200mg potassium.

Bacon-Wrapped Asparagus

INGREDIENTS:
- 12 asparagus spears, trimmed
- 6 slices of bacon
- 1/2 tsp garlic powder
- 1/4 tsp black pepper
- Cooking spray or olive oil

Prep Time: 5 min **Cook Time: 12 min** **Serves: 4**

DIRECTIONS:
1. Preheat the air fryer to 375°F (190°C). **2.** Divide asparagus into 6 bundles (2 spears per bundle). **3.** Wrap each bundle tightly with a slice of bacon. **4.** Lightly spray the wrapped asparagus with cooking spray or oil, and season with garlic powder and black pepper. **5.** Place the bundles in a single layer in the air fryer basket, ensuring they do not overlap. **6.** Cook for 10-12 minutes, flipping halfway through, until the bacon is crispy and the asparagus is tender. **7.** Let cool slightly before serving.

NUTRITIONAL INFORMATION
Per serving: 180 calories, 9g protein, 2g carbohydrates, 15g fat, 1g fiber, 25mg cholesterol, 400mg sodium, 150mg potassium.

Pepperoni Chips

INGREDIENTS:
- 24 slices of pepperoni
- Cooking spray or olive oil (optional)
- 1/4 tsp garlic powder (optional)
- 1/4 tsp paprika (optional)

Prep Time: 2 min **мCook Time: 7 min** **мServes: 4**

DIRECTIONS:
1. Preheat the air fryer to 350°F (175°C). **2.** Arrange the pepperoni slices in a single layer in the air fryer basket. **3.** Lightly spray with cooking spray or olive oil, if desired. Optionally, sprinkle garlic powder and paprika for added flavor. **4.** Air fry for 5-7 minutes until the pepperoni slices are crispy, shaking the basket halfway through for even cooking. **5.** Remove and place on paper towels to absorb any excess oil. Let cool slightly before serving.

NUTRITIONAL INFORMATION
Per serving: 150 calories, 6g protein, 1g carbohydrates, 13g fat, 0g fiber, 30mg cholesterol, 480mg sodium, 100mg potassium.

Air-Fried Cheese Sticks

INGREDIENTS:

- 8 mozzarella cheese sticks (string cheese)
- 1/2 cup almond flour
- 1/4 cup grated Parmesan cheese
- 1 large egg, beaten
- 1/2 tsp garlic powder
- 1/2 tsp Italian seasoning
- Salt and pepper to taste
- Cooking spray or olive oil

Prep Time: 10 min   **Cook Time: 8 min**   **Serves: 4**

DIRECTIONS:

1. Freeze the mozzarella sticks for at least 30 minutes to prevent melting during cooking. **2.** In one bowl, whisk the egg. In another, mix almond flour, Parmesan, garlic powder, Italian seasoning, salt, and pepper. **3.** Dip each frozen cheese stick in the egg, then coat with the almond flour mixture. Repeat for a thicker coating. **4.** Preheat the air fryer to 375°F (190°C). **5.** Lightly spray the air fryer basket with cooking spray. **6.** Place cheese sticks in a single layer in the basket and cook for 6-8 minutes until golden and crispy, flipping halfway through.

NUTRITIONAL INFORMATION

Per serving: 250 calories, 15g protein, 3g carbohydrates, 20g fat, 1g fiber, 60mg cholesterol, 450mg sodium, 100mg potassium.

Garlic Parmesan Broccoli Bites

INGREDIENTS:

- 2 cups broccoli florets
- 1/4 cup grated Parmesan cheese
- 2 tbsp olive oil
- 2 cloves garlic, minced
- 1/2 tsp garlic powder
- 1/4 tsp paprika
- Salt and pepper to taste
- Cooking spray

Prep Time: 5 min   **Cook Time: 12 min**   **Serves: 4**

DIRECTIONS:

1. In a bowl, toss broccoli florets with olive oil, garlic, Parmesan, garlic powder, paprika, salt, and pepper until evenly coated. **2.** Preheat the air fryer to 375°F (190°C). **3.** Lightly spray the air fryer basket with cooking spray. **4.** Place the broccoli in the basket in a single layer. **5.** Air fry for 10-12 minutes, shaking the basket halfway through, until the broccoli is tender and crispy at the edges. **6.** Remove from the air fryer and let cool slightly before serving.

NUTRITIONAL INFORMATION

Per serving: 120 calories, 5g protein, 4g carbohydrates, 10g fat, 2g fiber, 5mg cholesterol, 180mg sodium, 250mg potassium.

Keto Deviled Eggs

Prep Time: 5 min   **Cook Time: 15 min**   ᴍServes: 3

INGREDIENTS:

- 6 large eggs
- 1/4 cup mayonnaise
- 1 tsp Dijon mustard
- 1/2 tsp apple cider vinegar
- 1/4 tsp paprika
- Salt and pepper to taste
- Fresh chives or bacon bits for garnish (optional)
- Cooking spray

DIRECTIONS:

1. Preheat the air fryer to 270°F (130°C). **2.** Place the eggs in the air fryer basket, ensuring they don't touch. **3.** Cook for 15 minutes. Once done, transfer eggs to an ice bath to cool for 5-10 minutes. **4.** Peel the eggs and slice them in half lengthwise. **5.** Scoop out the yolks and place them in a bowl. Mash with mayonnaise, mustard, vinegar, paprika, salt, and pepper until smooth. **6.** Fill each egg white with the yolk mixture. **7.** Garnish with chives or bacon bits if desired.

NUTRITIONAL INFORMATION

Per serving (2 eggs): 180 calories, 7g protein, 1g carbohydrates, 15g fat, 0g fiber, 190mg cholesterol, 180mg sodium, 70mg potassium.

Chicken Nuggets with Almond Crust

Prep Time: 10 min   **Cook Time: 12 min**   **Serves: 4**

INGREDIENTS:

- 1 lb chicken breast, cut into bite-sized pieces
- 1/2 cup almond flour
- 1/4 cup grated Parmesan cheese
- 1 large egg, beaten
- 1/2 tsp garlic powder
- 1/2 tsp paprika
- Salt and pepper to taste
- Cooking spray or olive oil

DIRECTIONS:

1. Preheat the air fryer to 375°F (190°C). **2.** In one bowl, whisk the egg. In another bowl, combine almond flour, Parmesan, garlic powder, paprika, salt, and pepper. **3.** Dip each chicken piece into the egg, then coat with the almond flour mixture. **4.** Lightly grease the air fryer basket with cooking spray. **5.** Place the chicken nuggets in a single layer in the basket. Cook for 10-12 minutes, flipping halfway through, until crispy and golden, and the chicken is cooked through (internal temp should reach 165°F). **6.** Let the nuggets cool slightly before serving.

NUTRITIONAL INFORMATION

Per serving: 290 calories, 28g protein, 3g carbohydrates, 18g fat, 2g fiber, 100mg cholesterol, 350mg sodium, 320mg potassium.

Crispy Kale Chips

INGREDIENTS:

- 1 bunch kale, stems removed and torn into bite-sized pieces
- 1 tbsp olive oil
- 1/4 tsp garlic powder
- 1/4 tsp paprika (optional)
- Salt and pepper to taste
- Cooking spray

Prep Time: 5 min

Cook Time: 7 min

мServes: 4

DIRECTIONS:

1. Preheat the air fryer to 350°F (175°C). **2.** In a bowl, toss kale with olive oil, garlic powder, paprika (if using), salt, and pepper until evenly coated. **3.** Lightly spray the air fryer basket with cooking spray. **4.** Place kale in the basket in a single layer, ensuring they don't overlap. **5.** Air fry for 5-7 minutes, shaking the basket halfway through for even cooking, until crispy and slightly browned. **6.** Remove kale chips from the air fryer and let cool for a few minutes before serving.

NUTRITIONAL INFORMATION

Per serving: 70 calories, 2g protein, 4g carbohydrates, 5g fat, 1g fiber, 0mg cholesterol, 70mg sodium, 150mg potassium.

Fried Pickles with Ranch Dip

INGREDIENTS:

- For Fried Pickles:
- 12 dill pickle slices (or spears)
- 1/2 cup almond flour
- 1/4 cup grated Parmesan cheese
- 1 large egg, beaten
- 1/2 tsp garlic powder
- 1/2 tsp paprika
- Salt and pepper to taste
- Cooking spray or olive oil
-
- For Ranch Dip:
- 1/4 cup mayonnaise
- 1/4 cup sour cream
- 1/2 tsp dried dill
- 1/2 tsp garlic powder
- 1/2 tsp onion powder
- Salt and pepper to taste

Prep Time: 10 min

Cook Time: 10 min

Serves: 4

DIRECTIONS:

1. Pat pickles dry with paper towels. **2.** Mix almond flour, Parmesan, garlic powder, paprika, salt, and pepper in one bowl. In another, whisk the egg. **3.** Dip each pickle slice into the egg, then coat with the almond flour mixture. **4.** Preheat the air fryer to 375°F (190°C). **5.** Lightly spray the air fryer basket and place the coated pickles in a single layer. **6.** Air fry for 8-10 minutes, flipping halfway through until crispy and golden. **7.** Mix all ranch dip ingredients in a bowl.

NUTRITIONAL INFORMATION

Per serving: 210 calories, 7g protein, 4g carbohydrates, 18g fat, 2g fiber, 60mg cholesterol, 550mg sodium, 150mg potassium.

Air-Fried Tofu Bites

INGREDIENTS:

- 200g firm tofu, cubed
- 2 tbsp olive oil
- 1 tsp soy sauce (or tamari for gluten-free)
- 1/2 tsp garlic powder
- 1/2 tsp paprika
- 1/4 tsp salt
- 1/4 tsp black pepper
- Optional: 1 tbsp sesame seeds

мPrep Time: 5 min   Cook Time: 12 min   мServes: 2

DIRECTIONS:

1. Preheat the air fryer to 375°F (190°C). **2.** Toss tofu cubes with olive oil, soy sauce, garlic powder, paprika, salt, and pepper. **3.** Place tofu in the air fryer basket in a single layer. **4.** Cook at 375°F (190°C) for 10-12 minutes, shaking the basket halfway through. **5.** Tip: Ensure even spacing for crispier bites.

Serving Suggestion: Serve with a side of avocado dip or low-carb dressing.

NUTRITIONAL INFORMATION

180 calories, 9g protein, 3g carbohydrates, 14g fat, 1g fiber, 0mg cholesterol, 320mg sodium, 150mg potassium.

Cucumber Bites with Cream Cheese

INGREDIENTS:

- 1 large cucumber, sliced into thick rounds
- 100g cream cheese, softened
- 1 tbsp olive oil
- 1/2 tsp garlic powder
- 1/4 tsp salt
- 1/4 tsp black pepper
- Optional: 1 tbsp chopped fresh dill or chives

Prep Time: 5 min   Cook Time: 8 min   Serves: 4

DIRECTIONS:

1. Preheat the air fryer to 350°F (180°C). **2.** Brush cucumber slices with olive oil, sprinkle with garlic powder, salt, and pepper. **3.** Air fry at 350°F (180°C) for 5 minutes, then cool slightly. **4.** Spread cream cheese on each slice, sprinkle with dill or chives. **5.** Tip: Cook cucumber in a single layer for even crisping.

Serving Suggestion: Serve chilled with smoked salmon or olives.

NUTRITIONAL INFORMATION

140 calories, 3g protein, 4g carbohydrates, 12g fat, 1g fiber, 30mg cholesterol, 160mg sodium, 100mg potassium.

Keto Stuffed Mini Bell Peppers

INGREDIENTS:

- 10 mini bell peppers, halved and seeded
- 100g cream cheese, softened
- 1/4 cup shredded cheddar cheese
- 50g cooked bacon bits
- 1/4 tsp garlic powder
- 1/4 tsp black pepper
- Optional: 1 tbsp chopped fresh parsley

Prep Time: 5 min   **Cook Time: 10 min**   **Serves: 4**

DIRECTIONS:

1. Preheat the air fryer to 360°F (180°C). **2.** Mix cream cheese, cheddar, bacon, garlic powder, and pepper in a bowl. **3.** Stuff each mini bell pepper half with the cheese mixture. **4.** Arrange peppers in the air fryer basket in a single layer. **5.** Cook at 360°F (180°C) for 8-10 minutes, shaking halfway for even cooking.

Serving Suggestion: Serve warm with a side of avocado dip or fresh herbs.

NUTRITIONAL INFORMATION

180 calories, 6g protein, 4g carbohydrates, 16g fat, 1g fiber, 30mg cholesterol, 220mg sodium, 120mg potassium.

Bacon-Wrapped Jalapeño Poppers

INGREDIENTS:

- 6 large jalapeños, halved and seeded
- 100g cream cheese, softened
- 1/4 cup shredded cheddar cheese
- 6 strips of bacon, cut in half
- 1/4 tsp garlic powder
- 1/4 tsp black pepper
- Optional: 1 tbsp chopped chives

Prep Time: 5 min   **Cook Time: 12 min**   **Serves: 4**

DIRECTIONS:

1. Preheat the air fryer to 370°F (190°C). **2.** Mix cream cheese, cheddar, garlic powder, and pepper in a bowl. **3.** Fill each jalapeño half with the cheese mixture. **4.** Wrap each stuffed jalapeño with bacon, securing with a toothpick. **5.** Cook in the air fryer at 370°F (190°C) for 10-12 minutes, flipping halfway for even crisping.

Serving Suggestion: Serve hot with a side of ranch dressing or sour cream.

NUTRITIONAL INFORMATION

210 calories, 8g protein, 2g carbohydrates, 19g fat, 0.5g fiber, 30mg cholesterol, 350mg sodium, 150mg potassium.

Zucchini Fritters with Sour Cream Dip

INGREDIENTS:

- 1 medium zucchini, grated and drained
- 1/4 cup almond flour
- 1 large egg
- 2 tbsp grated Parmesan cheese
- 1/4 tsp garlic powder
- 1/4 tsp salt
- 1/4 tsp black pepper
- Optional: 1 tbsp chopped fresh parsley
- 1/4 cup sour cream (for dipping)

Prep Time: 10 min   **Cook Time: 12 min**   **Serves: 4**

DIRECTIONS:

1. Preheat the air fryer to 360°F (180°C). **2.** Mix zucchini, almond flour, egg, Parmesan, garlic powder, salt, and pepper. **3.** Form small patties and place in a single layer in the air fryer basket. **4.** Cook at 360°F (180°C) for 10-12 minutes, flipping halfway for even browning.
Serving Suggestion: Serve warm with sour cream dip and garnish with parsley.

NUTRITIONAL INFORMATION

120 calories, 5g protein, 4g carbohydrates, 9g fat, 1g fiber, 40mg cholesterol, 180mg sodium, 180mg potassium.

Cheese-Stuffed Bacon-Wrapped Jalapeños

INGREDIENTS:

- 6 large jalapeños, halved and seeded
- 100g cream cheese, softened
- 1/4 cup shredded cheddar cheese
- 6 slices of bacon, cut in half
- 1/4 tsp garlic powder
- 1/4 tsp black pepper
- Optional: 1 tbsp chopped chives

Prep Time: 5 min   **Cook Time: 12 min**   **Serves: 4**

DIRECTIONS:

1. Preheat the air fryer to 370°F (190°C). **2.** Mix cream cheese, cheddar, garlic powder, and pepper in a bowl. **3.** Fill each jalapeño half with the cheese mixture. **4.** Wrap each stuffed jalapeño with bacon, securing with a toothpick. **5.** Cook at 370°F (190°C) for 10-12 minutes, flipping halfway for even crisping.
Serving Suggestion: Serve hot with a side of sour cream or ranch dressing.

NUTRITIONAL INFORMATION

230 calories, 8g protein, 2g carbohydrates, 20g fat, 0.5g fiber, 30mg cholesterol, 360mg sodium, 150mg potassium.

Lemon Garlic Chicken Thighs

INGREDIENTS:

- 4 bone-in, skin-on chicken thighs
- 2 tbsp olive oil
- 2 tbsp lemon juice
- 2 cloves garlic, minced
- 1 tsp lemon zest
- 1 tsp dried thyme
- 1/2 tsp paprika
- Salt and pepper to taste
- Cooking spray or olive oil

мPrep Time: 10 min   Cook Time: 25 min   Serves: 4

DIRECTIONS:

1. In a bowl, mix olive oil, lemon juice, garlic, lemon zest, thyme, paprika, salt, and pepper. **2.** Coat the chicken thighs in the marinade and let sit for 15 minutes (optional for better flavor). **3.** Preheat the air fryer to 375°F (190°C). **4.** Lightly spray the air fryer basket with cooking spray. **5.** Place chicken thighs in the basket skin-side down. Air fry for 10-12 minutes, then flip and cook for an additional 10-12 minutes, until the skin is crispy and the internal temperature reaches 165°F. **6.** Let the chicken rest for 5 minutes before serving.

NUTRITIONAL INFORMATION

Per serving: 320 calories, 24g protein, 2g carbohydrates, 24g fat, 0g fiber, 110mg cholesterol, 420mg sodium, 260mg potassium.

Keto Air Fryer Chicken Tenders

INGREDIENTS:

- 1 lb chicken tenders
- 1/2 cup almond flour
- 1/4 cup grated Parmesan cheese
- 1 large egg, beaten
- 1/2 tsp garlic powder
- 1/2 tsp paprika
- Salt and pepper to taste
- Cooking spray or olive oil

Prep Time: 10 min   Cook Time: 12 min   Serves: 4

DIRECTIONS:

1. In one bowl, beat the egg. In another, mix almond flour, Parmesan, garlic powder, paprika, salt, and pepper. **2.** Dip each chicken tender in the egg, then coat with the almond flour mixture. **3.** Preheat the air fryer to 375°F (190°C). **4.** Lightly spray the air fryer basket with cooking spray. **5.** Place the chicken tenders in a single layer in the basket. Air fry for 10-12 minutes, flipping halfway through, until golden brown and the internal temperature reaches 165°F. **6.** Let the tenders rest for a few minutes before serving.

NUTRITIONAL INFORMATION

Per serving: 280 calories, 25g protein, 3g carbohydrates, 18g fat, 1g fiber, 100mg cholesterol, 380mg sodium, 250mg potassium.

Bacon-Wrapped Chicken Breast

INGREDIENTS:

- 2 boneless, skinless chicken breasts
- 4 slices bacon
- 1/2 tsp garlic powder
- 1/2 tsp paprika
- 1/4 tsp black pepper
- Salt to taste
- Cooking spray or olive oil

Prep Time: 5 min   **Cook Time: 18 min**   **Serves: 2**

DIRECTIONS:

1. Preheat the air fryer to 375°F (190°C). **2.** Season the chicken breasts with garlic powder, paprika, salt, and pepper. **3.** Wrap each chicken breast with 2 slices of bacon, ensuring the ends are tucked underneath or secured with toothpicks. **4.** Lightly spray the air fryer basket with cooking spray or oil. **5.** Place the bacon-wrapped chicken breasts in a single layer in the basket. **6.** Cook for 15-18 minutes, flipping halfway through, until the bacon is crispy and the internal temperature of the chicken reaches 165°F. **7.** Let rest for a few minutes before serving.

NUTRITIONAL INFORMATION

Per serving: 360 calories, 40g protein, 2g carbohydrates, 20g fat, 0g fiber, 120mg cholesterol, 700mg sodium, 300mg potassium.

Crispy Chicken Parmesan

INGREDIENTS:

- 2 boneless, skinless chicken breasts
- 1/2 cup almond flour
- 1/4 cup grated Parmesan cheese
- 1 large egg, beaten
- 1/2 tsp garlic powder
- 1/2 tsp Italian seasoning
- 1/4 cup marinara sauce (sugar-free)
- 1/4 cup shredded mozzarella cheese
- Salt and pepper to taste
- Cooking spray or olive oil

Prep Time: 10 min   **Cook Time: 15 min**   **Serves: 2**

DIRECTIONS:

1. Preheat air fryer to 375°F (190°C). **2.** Season chicken breasts with salt and pepper. **3.** In one bowl, whisk the egg. In another, mix almond flour, Parmesan, garlic powder, and Italian seasoning. **4.** Dip each chicken breast in the egg, then coat with the almond flour mixture. **5.** Lightly spray the air fryer basket and place chicken in a single layer. **6.** Air fry for 10-12 minutes, flipping halfway through. **7.** Top each chicken breast with marinara sauce and mozzarella cheese. Air fry for an additional 2-3 minutes until cheese is melted.

NUTRITIONAL INFORMATION

Per serving: 390 calories, 40g protein, 5g carbohydrates, 23g fat, 2g fiber, 120mg cholesterol, 650mg sodium, 350mg potassium.

Buffalo Chicken Drumsticks

INGREDIENTS:

- 6 chicken drumsticks
- 1/4 cup olive oil
- 1/2 tsp garlic powder
- 1/2 tsp paprika
- Salt and pepper to taste
- 1/4 cup buffalo sauce (sugar-free)
- 2 tbsp unsalted butter, melted

Prep Time: 5 min   **Cook Time: 25 min**   **Serves: 3**

DIRECTIONS:

1. Preheat the air fryer to 375°F (190°C). **2.** In a bowl, mix olive oil, garlic powder, paprika, salt, and pepper. Coat the drumsticks with the mixture. **3.** Place the drumsticks in the air fryer basket in a single layer. **4.** Cook for 20-25 minutes, flipping halfway through, until crispy and the internal temperature reaches 165°F. **5.** While cooking, mix buffalo sauce and melted butter. **6.** Once the drumsticks are done, toss them in the buffalo sauce mixture.

NUTRITIONAL INFORMATION

Per serving: 320 calories, 27g protein, 2g carbohydrates, 23g fat, 0g fiber, 120mg cholesterol, 520mg sodium, 350mg potassium.

Cajun-Spiced Chicken Wings

INGREDIENTS:

- 2 lbs chicken wings
- 2 tbsp olive oil
- 1 tbsp Cajun seasoning
- 1/2 tsp garlic powder
- 1/2 tsp smoked paprika
- Salt and pepper to taste
- Cooking spray or olive oil

Prep Time: 5 min   **Cook Time: 25 min**   **Serves: 4**

DIRECTIONS:

1. Preheat the air fryer to 375°F (190°C). **2.** In a bowl, toss the chicken wings with olive oil, Cajun seasoning, garlic powder, smoked paprika, salt, and pepper. **3.** Lightly spray the air fryer basket with cooking spray. **4.** Place the seasoned wings in a single layer in the basket. **5.** Cook for 20-25 minutes, flipping the wings halfway through, until crispy and the internal temperature reaches 165°F. **6.** Shake the basket or flip the wings midway to ensure even cooking.

NUTRITIONAL INFORMATION

Per serving: 290 calories, 24g protein, 1g carbohydrates, 21g fat, 0g fiber, 100mg cholesterol, 480mg sodium, 250mg potassium.

Keto Chicken Nuggets

INGREDIENTS:

- 1 lb chicken breast, cut into bite-sized pieces
- 1/2 cup almond flour
- 1/4 cup grated Parmesan cheese
- 1 large egg, beaten
- 1/2 tsp garlic powder
- 1/2 tsp paprika
- Salt and pepper to taste
- Cooking spray or olive oil

Prep Time: 10 min   **Cook Time: 12 min**   **Serves: 4**

DIRECTIONS:

1. Preheat the air fryer to 375°F (190°C). **2.** In a bowl, mix almond flour, Parmesan cheese, garlic powder, paprika, salt, and pepper. **3.** In a separate bowl, whisk the egg. **4.** Dip each chicken piece into the egg, then coat with the almond flour mixture. **5.** Lightly spray the air fryer basket with cooking spray or olive oil. **6.** Place the chicken nuggets in a single layer in the basket. **7.** Cook for 10-12 minutes, flipping halfway through, until golden and crispy, and the internal temperature reaches 165°F.

NUTRITIONAL INFORMATION

Per serving: 250 calories, 28g protein, 3g carbohydrates, 14g fat, 1g fiber, 95mg cholesterol, 300mg sodium, 250mg potassium.

Air Fryer Turkey Meatballs

INGREDIENTS:

- 1 lb ground turkey
- 1/4 cup almond flour
- 1/4 cup grated Parmesan cheese
- 1 large egg
- 1/2 tsp garlic powder
- 1/2 tsp onion powder
- 1 tsp Italian seasoning
- Salt and pepper to taste
- Cooking spray or olive oil

Prep Time: 10 min   **мCook Time: 12 min**   **Serves: 4**

DIRECTIONS:

1. Preheat the air fryer to 375°F (190°C). **2.** In a large bowl, combine ground turkey, almond flour, Parmesan, egg, garlic powder, onion powder, Italian seasoning, salt, and pepper. **3.** Form the mixture into 12 meatballs. **4.** Lightly spray the air fryer basket with cooking spray. **5.** Place the meatballs in the basket in a single layer. **6.** Cook for 10-12 minutes, shaking the basket halfway through, until the meatballs are golden and the internal temperature reaches 165°F.

NUTRITIONAL INFORMATION

Per serving: 220 calories, 26g protein, 3g carbohydrates, 12g fat, 1g fiber, 80mg cholesterol, 350mg sodium, 300mg potassium.

Chicken and Cheese Stuffed Bell Peppers

INGREDIENTS:

- 4 large bell peppers, halved and seeds removed
- 1 lb cooked, shredded chicken
- 1/2 cup shredded mozzarella cheese
- 1/2 cup cream cheese, softened
- 1/4 cup grated Parmesan cheese
- 1/2 tsp garlic powder
- 1/2 tsp paprika
- Salt and pepper to taste
- Cooking spray or olive oil

Prep Time: 10 min   **мCook Time: 12 min**   **Serves: 4**

DIRECTIONS:

1. Preheat the air fryer to 350°F (175°C). **2.** In a bowl, mix shredded chicken, cream cheese, mozzarella, Parmesan, garlic powder, paprika, salt, and pepper until well combined. **3.** Stuff each bell pepper half with the chicken and cheese mixture. **4.** Lightly spray the air fryer basket with cooking spray. **5.** Place stuffed bell peppers in the basket in a single layer. **6.** Air fry for 10-12 minutes, until the peppers are tender and the cheese is melted and golden.

NUTRITIONAL INFORMATION

Per serving: 350 calories, 30g protein, 6g carbohydrates, 22g fat, 2g fiber, 80mg cholesterol, 450mg sodium, 350mg potassium.

Herb-Crusted Turkey Breast

INGREDIENTS:

- 1 lb turkey breast, boneless and skinless
- 2 tbsp olive oil
- 1 tbsp fresh rosemary, chopped (or 1 tsp dried)
- 1 tbsp fresh thyme, chopped (or 1 tsp dried)
- 1 tsp garlic powder
- 1/2 tsp onion powder
- 1/2 tsp paprika
- Salt and pepper to taste
- Cooking spray or olive oil

Prep Time: 10 min   **Cook Time: 25 min**   **Serves: 4**

DIRECTIONS:

1. Preheat the air fryer to 375°F (190°C). **2.** In a bowl, mix olive oil, rosemary, thyme, garlic powder, onion powder, paprika, salt, and pepper. **3.** Rub the herb mixture evenly over the turkey breast. **4.** Lightly spray the air fryer basket with cooking spray. **5.** Place the turkey breast in the basket and cook for 20-25 minutes, flipping halfway through, until the internal temperature reaches 165°F. **6.** Let the turkey rest for 5 minutes before slicing.

NUTRITIONAL INFORMATION

Per serving: 250 calories, 32g protein, 1g carbohydrates, 13g fat, 0g fiber, 80mg cholesterol, 300mg sodium, 400mg potassium.

Air-Fried Duck Confit

INGREDIENTS:
- 4 duck legs, skin on
- 2 tbsp duck fat or olive oil
- 1 tbsp fresh thyme (or 1 tsp dried)
- 1 tbsp fresh rosemary (or 1 tsp dried)
- 4 garlic cloves, minced
- Salt and pepper to taste

Prep Time: 10 min   **Cook Time: 30 min**   **Serves: 4**

DIRECTIONS:
1. Rub the duck legs with salt, pepper, thyme, rosemary, and minced garlic. Let the legs rest for 1 hour to enhance flavor. **2.** Preheat the air fryer to 375°F (190°C). **3.** Rub each duck leg with duck fat or olive oil. **4.** Place the duck legs in the air fryer basket, skin-side up, in a single layer. **5.** Cook for 25-30 minutes, flipping halfway through, until the skin is crispy and the internal temperature reaches 165°F. **6.** Let rest for 5 minutes before serving.

NUTRITIONAL INFORMATION
Per serving: 400 calories, 30g protein, 0g carbohydrates, 30g fat, 0g fiber, 120mg cholesterol, 500mg sodium, 300mg potassium.

Spicy Chicken Satay

INGREDIENTS:
- 1 lb chicken breast, cut into strips
- 2 tbsp coconut aminos (or soy sauce alternative)
- 1 tbsp olive oil
- 1 tbsp lime juice
- 1 tsp garlic powder
- 1 tsp ground cumin
- 1/2 tsp chili powder (adjust for spice level)
- 1/2 tsp turmeric
- Salt and pepper to taste
- Bamboo skewers, soaked in water

Prep Time: 10 min   **Cook Time: 12 min**   **Serves: 4**

DIRECTIONS:
1. In a bowl, mix coconut aminos, olive oil, lime juice, garlic powder, cumin, chili powder, turmeric, salt, and pepper. 2. Marinate the chicken strips in the mixture for at least 30 minutes. **3.** Preheat the air fryer to 375°F (190°C). **4.** Thread the marinated chicken onto soaked skewers. **5.** Place the skewers in a single layer in the air fryer basket. **6.** Air fry for 10-12 minutes, flipping halfway, until the chicken is fully cooked (internal temperature 165°F).

NUTRITIONAL INFORMATION
Per serving: 220 calories, 26g protein, 2g carbohydrates, 12g fat, 0g fiber, 70mg cholesterol, 500mg sodium, 300mg potassium.

Lemon Pepper Chicken Wings

INGREDIENTS:

- 2 lbs chicken wings
- 2 tbsp olive oil
- 1 tbsp lemon zest
- 1 tsp garlic powder
- 1 tsp onion powder
- 1 tsp black pepper
- 1/2 tsp salt
- 1 tbsp fresh lemon juice
- Cooking spray or olive oil

Prep Time: 5 min   **Cook Time: 25 min**   **Serves: 4**

DIRECTIONS:

1. Preheat the air fryer to 375°F (190°C). **2.** In a bowl, toss the chicken wings with olive oil, lemon zest, garlic powder, onion powder, black pepper, and salt. **3.** Lightly spray the air fryer basket with cooking spray. **4.** Place wings in a single layer in the basket. **5.** Cook for 20-25 minutes, shaking the basket halfway through, until wings are crispy and cooked through (internal temperature should reach 165°F). **6.** Toss the cooked wings in fresh lemon juice before serving.

NUTRITIONAL INFORMATION

Per serving: 300 calories, 24g protein, 1g carbohydrates, 22g fat, 0g fiber, 100mg cholesterol, 480mg sodium, 300mg potassium.

Air-Fried Chicken Fajitas

INGREDIENTS:

- 1 lb chicken breast, sliced into strips
- 1 bell pepper, sliced
- 1 small onion, sliced
- 2 tbsp olive oil
- 1 tsp chili powder
- 1 tsp cumin
- 1/2 tsp garlic powder
- 1/2 tsp paprika
- Salt and pepper to taste
- Cooking spray

Prep Time: 10 min   **Cook Time: 15 min**   **Serves: 4**

DIRECTIONS:

1. Preheat the air fryer to 375°F (190°C). **2.** In a bowl, combine olive oil, chili powder, cumin, garlic powder, paprika, salt, and pepper. **3.** Toss chicken strips, bell pepper, and onion in the spice mixture to coat evenly. **4.** Lightly spray the air fryer basket with cooking spray. **5.** Place chicken and vegetables in the basket in a single layer. **6.** Cook for 12-15 minutes, shaking the basket halfway through, until the chicken is cooked through (internal temperature reaches 165°F) and the vegetables are tender.

NUTRITIONAL INFORMATION

Per serving: 280 calories, 26g protein, 5g carbohydrates, 17g fat, 1g fiber, 75mg cholesterol, 320mg sodium, 400mg potassium.

Bacon-Wrapped Turkey Roll-Ups

INGREDIENTS:

- 8 thin slices of turkey breast (deli-style or pounded thin)
- 8 slices bacon
- 4 oz cream cheese, softened
- 1/2 tsp garlic powder
- 1/2 tsp dried thyme
- Salt and pepper to taste
- Cooking spray or olive oil

Prep Time: 10 min   мCook Time: 15 min   **Serves: 4**

DIRECTIONS:

1. Preheat the air fryer to 375°F (190°C). **2.** In a bowl, mix cream cheese, garlic powder, thyme, salt, and pepper. **3.** Spread a thin layer of the cream cheese mixture onto each turkey slice. **4.** Roll each turkey slice tightly and wrap a slice of bacon around each roll-up. **5.** Lightly spray the air fryer basket with cooking spray. **6.** Place the turkey roll-ups in the air fryer basket in a single layer. **7.** Cook for 12-15 minutes, flipping halfway, until the bacon is crispy and the turkey is heated through.

NUTRITIONAL INFORMATION

Per serving: 300 calories, 20g protein, 2g carbohydrates, 23g fat, 0g fiber, 60mg cholesterol, 600mg sodium, 350mg potassium.

Chicken Thighs with Creamy Garlic Sauce

INGREDIENTS:

- 4 bone-in, skin-on chicken thighs
- 2 tbsp olive oil
- 1 tsp garlic powder
- 1/2 tsp paprika
- Salt and pepper to taste
-
- For Creamy Garlic Sauce:
- 1/4 cup heavy cream
- 2 tbsp butter
- 3 cloves garlic, minced
- 1/4 cup grated Parmesan cheese
- 1/2 tsp dried thyme
- Salt and pepper to taste

мPrep Time: 10 min   Cook Time: 25 min   **Serves: 4**

DIRECTIONS:

1. Preheat the air fryer to 375°F (190°C). **2.** Rub the chicken thighs with olive oil, garlic powder, paprika, salt, and pepper. **3.** Place the chicken thighs skin-side up in the air fryer basket and cook for 20-25 minutes, flipping halfway through, until the internal temperature reaches 165°F. **4.** In a small saucepan, melt butter over medium heat, add garlic, and sauté for 1 minute. **5.** Stir in heavy cream, Parmesan, thyme, salt, and pepper. Simmer for 2-3 minutes until thickened.

NUTRITIONAL INFORMATION

Per serving: 450 calories, 28g protein, 3g carbohydrates, 36g fat, 0g fiber, 120mg cholesterol, 520mg sodium, 350mg potassium.

Crispy Pesto Chicken

INGREDIENTS:

- 4 boneless, skinless chicken breasts
- 1/4 cup pesto (store-bought or homemade)
- 1/2 cup almond flour
- 1/4 cup grated Parmesan cheese
- 1 large egg, beaten
- 1/2 tsp garlic powder
- Salt and pepper to taste
- Cooking spray or olive oil

Prep Time: 10 min   **Cook Time: 15 min**   **Serves: 4**

DIRECTIONS:

1. Preheat the air fryer to 375°F (190°C). **2.** Rub each chicken breast with a tablespoon of pesto and let it sit for 5 minutes. **3.** In one bowl, whisk the egg. In another bowl, mix almond flour, Parmesan, garlic powder, salt, and pepper. **4.** Dip each pesto-coated chicken breast in the egg, then coat with the almond flour mixture. **5.** Lightly spray the air fryer basket with cooking spray. **6.** Place chicken in a single layer in the air fryer basket. Cook for 12-15 minutes, flipping halfway through, until the chicken is crispy and reaches an internal temperature of 165°F.

NUTRITIONAL INFORMATION

Per serving: 350 calories, 35g protein, 3g carbohydrates, 22g fat, 1g fiber, 120mg cholesterol, 450mg sodium, 350mg potassium.

Air-Fried Chicken Cordon Bleu

INGREDIENTS:

- 4 boneless, skinless chicken breasts
- 4 slices Swiss cheese
- 4 slices ham (sugar-free, keto-friendly)
- 1/2 cup almond flour
- 1/4 cup grated Parmesan cheese
- 1 large egg, beaten
- 1/2 tsp garlic powder
- 1/2 tsp paprika
- Salt and pepper to taste
- Cooking spray or olive oil

Prep Time: 15 min   **Cook Time: 18 min**   **Serves: 4**

DIRECTIONS:

1. Preheat the air fryer to 375°F (190°C). **2.** Butterfly each chicken breast and place a slice of ham and Swiss cheese inside, then fold the chicken over to seal. **3.** In one bowl, beat the egg. In another, mix almond flour, Parmesan, garlic powder, paprika, salt, and pepper. **4.** Dip each chicken breast in the egg, then coat with the almond flour mixture. **5.** Lightly spray the air fryer basket with cooking spray. **6.** Place chicken breasts in the basket and cook for 15-18 minutes, flipping halfway through, until golden and the internal temperature reaches 165°F.

NUTRITIONAL INFORMATION

Per serving: 410 calories, 45g protein, 4g carbohydrates, 23g fat, 1g fiber, 130mg cholesterol, 600mg sodium, 450mg potassium.

Stuffed Chicken Breast with Spinach and Feta

INGREDIENTS:

- 2 large chicken breasts
- 1/2 cup spinach, chopped
- 1/4 cup feta cheese, crumbled
- 1 tbsp olive oil
- 1/4 tsp garlic powder
- 1/4 tsp black pepper
- 1/4 tsp salt
- Optional: 1 tbsp sun-dried tomatoes, chopped

Prep Time: 10 min   **Cook Time: 15 min**   **Serves: 2**

DIRECTIONS:

1. Preheat the air fryer to 375°F (190°C). **2.** Slice a pocket into each chicken breast. **3.** Mix spinach, feta, garlic powder, and optional tomatoes; stuff into the chicken. **4.** Brush chicken with olive oil, sprinkle with salt and pepper. **5.** Cook in the air fryer at 375°F (190°C) for 12-15 minutes, flipping halfway.

Serving Suggestion: Serve with a side of cauliflower rice or mixed greens.

NUTRITIONAL INFORMATION

310 calories, 34g protein, 2g carbohydrates, 18g fat, 1g fiber, 90mg cholesterol, 480mg sodium, 450mg potassium.

Honey Mustard Glazed Chicken Drumsticks

INGREDIENTS:

- 6 chicken drumsticks
- 2 tbsp Dijon mustard
- 1 tbsp sugar-free honey substitute
- 1 tbsp olive oil
- 1/2 tsp garlic powder
- 1/2 tsp paprika
- 1/4 tsp salt
- 1/4 tsp black pepper

Prep Time: 5 min   **Cook Time: 20 min**   **Serves: 3**

DIRECTIONS:

1. Preheat the air fryer to 380°F (190°C). **2.** Mix mustard, honey substitute, olive oil, garlic powder, paprika, salt, and pepper. **3.** Coat drumsticks with the glaze. **4.** Place drumsticks in the air fryer basket in a single layer. **5.** Cook at 380°F (190°C) for 18-20 minutes, flipping halfway through.

Serving Suggestion: Serve with a side of steamed broccoli or cauliflower mash.

NUTRITIONAL INFORMATION

250 calories, 22g protein, 2g carbohydrates, 17g fat, 0g fiber, 120mg cholesterol, 400mg sodium, 280mg potassium.

Garlic Butter Steak Bites

INGREDIENTS:
- 1 lb sirloin steak, cut into bite-sized pieces
- 2 tbsp olive oil
- 1/2 tsp garlic powder
- Salt and pepper to taste
- 2 tbsp butter, melted
- 3 cloves garlic, minced
- 1 tbsp fresh parsley, chopped (optional)

Prep Time: 5 min   **Cook Time: 10 min**   **Serves: 4**

DIRECTIONS:
1. Preheat the air fryer to 400°F (200°C). **2.** Toss steak bites in olive oil, garlic powder, salt, and pepper. **3.** Place steak bites in the air fryer basket in a single layer. **4.** Cook for 8-10 minutes, shaking the basket halfway through, until the steak reaches desired doneness (internal temp of 130°F for medium-rare). **5.** While cooking, mix melted butter with minced garlic. **6.** Toss the cooked steak bites in the garlic butter mixture and sprinkle with parsley if desired.

NUTRITIONAL INFORMATION
Per serving: 320 calories, 25g protein, 1g carbohydrates, 24g fat, 0g fiber, 80mg cholesterol, 300mg sodium, 400mg potassium.

Keto Meatballs with Marinara

INGREDIENTS:
- 1 lb ground beef (or turkey)
- 1/4 cup almond flour
- 1/4 cup grated Parmesan cheese
- 1 large egg
- 1 tsp garlic powder
- 1 tsp onion powder
- 1 tsp Italian seasoning
- Salt and pepper to taste
- 1 cup sugar-free marinara sauce
- Cooking spray or olive oil

Prep Time: 10 min   **Cook Time: 12 min**   **Serves: 4**

DIRECTIONS:
1. Preheat the air fryer to 375°F (190°C). **2.** In a bowl, combine ground meat, almond flour, Parmesan, egg, garlic powder, onion powder, Italian seasoning, salt, and pepper. **3.** Form the mixture into 12 meatballs. **4.** Lightly spray the air fryer basket with cooking spray. **5.** Place the meatballs in a single layer in the basket. **6.** Cook for 10-12 minutes, shaking the basket halfway through, until meatballs are golden and the internal temperature reaches 165°F. **7.** Heat the marinara sauce and serve over the meatballs.

NUTRITIONAL INFORMATION
Per serving: 290 calories, 24g protein, 4g carbohydrates, 20g fat, 1g fiber, 80mg cholesterol, 450mg sodium, 300mg potassium.

Crispy Beef Tacos

INGREDIENTS:

- 1 lb ground beef (80/20)
- 1 tsp chili powder
- 1/2 tsp cumin
- 1/2 tsp garlic powder
- 1/2 tsp onion powder
- Salt and pepper to taste
- 8 low-carb tortillas (keto-friendly)
- 1/2 cup shredded cheddar cheese
- Cooking spray or olive oil

Prep Time: 10 min **Cook Time: 12 min** мServes: 4

DIRECTIONS:

1. Preheat the air fryer to 375°F (190°C). **2.** In a skillet, cook ground beef over medium heat, adding chili powder, cumin, garlic powder, onion powder, salt, and pepper. Cook until browned. **3.** Lay out tortillas and fill each with beef and a sprinkle of cheddar cheese. **4.** Fold each tortilla in half and lightly spray with cooking spray or brush with olive oil. **5.** Place tacos in the air fryer basket in a single layer. **6.** Air fry for 5-7 minutes, flipping halfway through, until tortillas are crispy and golden.

NUTRITIONAL INFORMATION

Per serving: 320 calories, 24g protein, 4g carbohydrates, 23g fat, 2g fiber, 70mg cholesterol, 450mg sodium, 350mg potassium.

Herb-Crusted Lamb Chops

INGREDIENTS:

- 8 lamb chops (about 1 inch thick)
- 2 tbsp olive oil
- 1 tbsp fresh rosemary, chopped (or 1 tsp dried)
- 1 tbsp fresh thyme, chopped (or 1 tsp dried)
- 3 cloves garlic, minced
- 1/2 tsp salt
- 1/2 tsp black pepper

Prep Time: 10 min **Cook Time: 12 min** **Serves: 4**

DIRECTIONS:

1. Preheat the air fryer to 400°F (200°C). **2.** In a small bowl, mix olive oil, rosemary, thyme, garlic, salt, and pepper. **3.** Rub the herb mixture onto both sides of the lamb chops. **4.** Place lamb chops in the air fryer basket in a single layer. **5.** Air fry for 10-12 minutes, flipping halfway through, until the internal temperature reaches 145°F for medium-rare. **6.** Let rest for 5 minutes before serving.

NUTRITIONAL INFORMATION

Per serving: 420 calories, 30g protein, 1g carbohydrates, 33g fat, 0g fiber, 115mg cholesterol, 500mg sodium, 400mg potassium.

Bacon-Wrapped Pork Tenderloin

INGREDIENTS:

- 1 lb pork tenderloin
- 6-8 slices of bacon
- 2 tbsp olive oil
- 2 cloves garlic, minced
- 1 tsp paprika
- 1 tsp dried thyme
- Salt and pepper to taste
- Cooking spray or olive oil

мPrep Time: 10 min   Cook Time: 20 min   Serves: 4

DIRECTIONS:

1. Preheat the air fryer to 375°F (190°C). **2.** In a small bowl, mix olive oil, garlic, paprika, thyme, salt, and pepper. Rub this mixture all over the pork tenderloin. **3.** Wrap the bacon slices around the tenderloin, securing the ends with toothpicks if needed. **4.** Lightly spray the air fryer basket with cooking spray. **5.** Place the bacon-wrapped tenderloin in the basket and cook for 18-20 minutes, flipping halfway through, until the internal temperature reaches 145°F. **6.** Let rest for 5 minutes before slicing.

NUTRITIONAL INFORMATION

Per serving: 320 calories, 24g protein, 4g carbohydrates, 23g fat, 2g fiber, 70mg cholesterol, 450mg sodium, 350mg potassium.

Keto BBQ Ribs

INGREDIENTS:

- 1 rack of baby back ribs (about 1.5 lbs)
- 1 tbsp olive oil
- 1 tsp smoked paprika
- 1 tsp garlic powder
- 1 tsp onion powder
- 1/2 tsp cumin
- 1/2 tsp black pepper
- Salt to taste
- 1/4 cup sugar-free BBQ sauce

Prep Time: 10 min   Cook Time: 30 min   Serves: 4

DIRECTIONS:

1. Preheat the air fryer to 350°F (175°C). **2.** In a small bowl, mix olive oil, paprika, garlic powder, onion powder, cumin, black pepper, and salt. **3.** Rub the spice mixture evenly over the ribs. **4.** Cut the rack into smaller pieces (2-3 ribs per section) to fit in the air fryer. **5.** Place the ribs in the air fryer basket in a single layer. **6.** Cook for 25-30 minutes, flipping halfway through, until tender and cooked through. **7.** Brush ribs with sugar-free BBQ sauce in the last 5 minutes of cooking for a sticky glaze.

NUTRITIONAL INFORMATION

Per serving: 400 calories, 28g protein, 3g carbohydrates, 30g fat, 0g fiber, 100mg cholesterol, 550mg sodium, 450mg potassium.

Pork Belly Bites with Garlic Sauce

INGREDIENTS:

- 1 lb pork belly, cut into bite-sized cubes
- 1 tbsp olive oil
- 1 tsp smoked paprika
- 1/2 tsp garlic powder
- 1/2 tsp onion powder
- Salt and pepper to taste
-
- For Garlic Sauce:
- 2 tbsp butter
- 3 cloves garlic, minced
- 1 tbsp fresh lemon juice
- 1 tbsp fresh parsley, chopped (optional)
- Salt and pepper to taste

Prep Time: 10 min   **Cook Time: 20 min**   **Serves: 4**

DIRECTIONS:

1. Preheat the air fryer to 375°F (190°C). **2.** Toss pork belly cubes with olive oil, smoked paprika, garlic powder, onion powder, salt, and pepper. **3.** Place pork belly pieces in a single layer in the air fryer basket. **4.** Cook for 18-20 minutes, shaking the basket halfway through, until crispy and golden. **5.** While cooking, melt butter in a small saucepan over medium heat. Add minced garlic and sauté for 1-2 minutes until fragrant. Stir in lemon juice, parsley, salt, and pepper.

NUTRITIONAL INFORMATION

Per serving: 420 calories, 20g protein, 1g carbohydrates, 38g fat, 0g fiber, 80mg cholesterol, 500mg sodium, 300mg potassium.

Rosemary and Garlic Lamb Skewers

INGREDIENTS:

- 1 lb lamb, cut into bite-sized cubes
- 2 tbsp olive oil
- 2 cloves garlic, minced
- 1 tbsp fresh rosemary, chopped (or 1 tsp dried)
- 1 tsp lemon zest
- Salt and pepper to taste
- Wooden skewers, soaked in water for 30 minutes

Prep Time: 10 min   **Cook Time: 12 min**   **Serves: 4**

DIRECTIONS:

1. In a bowl, combine olive oil, minced garlic, rosemary, lemon zest, salt, and pepper. **2.** Toss the lamb cubes in the marinade and let sit for 15 minutes. **3.** Preheat the air fryer to 375°F (190°C). **4.** Thread the marinated lamb onto soaked skewers. **5.** Place the skewers in the air fryer basket in a single layer. **6.** Cook for 10-12 minutes, flipping halfway through, until lamb reaches desired doneness (internal temperature 145°F for medium-rare). **7.** Let the lamb rest for 5 minutes before serving.

NUTRITIONAL INFORMATION

Per serving: 310 calories, 24g protein, 1g carbohydrates, 23g fat, 0g fiber, 75mg cholesterol, 400mg sodium, 300mg potassium.

Air-Fried Pork Chops with Parmesan

INGREDIENTS:

- 4 boneless pork chops (1 inch thick)
- 1/2 cup grated Parmesan cheese
- 1/4 cup almond flour
- 1 tsp garlic powder
- 1/2 tsp paprika
- Salt and pepper to taste
- 1 large egg, beaten
- Cooking spray or olive oil

Prep Time: 10 min   **Cook Time: 15 min**   **Serves: 4**

DIRECTIONS:

1. Preheat the air fryer to 375°F (190°C). **2.** In one bowl, beat the egg. In another bowl, mix Parmesan, almond flour, garlic powder, paprika, salt, and pepper. **3.** Dip each pork chop in the beaten egg, then coat with the Parmesan mixture. **4.** Lightly spray the air fryer basket with cooking spray or olive oil. **5.** Place pork chops in a single layer in the basket. **6.** Air fry for 12-15 minutes, flipping halfway through, until golden and crispy, and the internal temperature reaches 145°F. **7.** Let the pork chops rest for 5 minutes before serving.

NUTRITIONAL INFORMATION

Per serving: 350 calories, 35g protein, 3g carbohydrates, 22g fat, 1g fiber, 95mg cholesterol, 400mg sodium, 500mg potassium.

Spicy Korean BBQ Beef

INGREDIENTS:

- 1 lb beef sirloin, thinly sliced
- 2 tbsp coconut aminos (or soy sauce alternative)
- 1 tbsp sesame oil
- 1 tbsp rice vinegar
- 1 tbsp gochugaru (Korean red pepper flakes) or chili powder
- 1 tsp garlic powder
- 1 tsp ginger powder
- 1 tsp sesame seeds (optional)
- 1 tsp sweetener (like erythritol or stevia)
- Cooking spray or olive oil

Prep Time: 10 min   **Cook Time: 10 min**   **Serves: 4**

DIRECTIONS:

1. In a bowl, mix coconut aminos, sesame oil, rice vinegar, gochugaru, garlic powder, ginger powder, sweetener, and sesame seeds. **2.** Add the thinly sliced beef to the marinade and let it sit for 15-20 minutes. **3.** Preheat the air fryer to 375°F (190°C). **4.** Lightly spray the air fryer basket with cooking spray or oil. **5.** Place the marinated beef in the air fryer basket in a single layer. **6.** Cook for 8-10 minutes, shaking the basket halfway through, until the beef is crispy on the edges and fully cooked.

NUTRITIONAL INFORMATION

Per serving: 270 calories, 25g protein, 3g carbohydrates, 17g fat, 0g fiber, 70mg cholesterol, 450mg sodium, 350mg potassium.

Keto Beef Stir-Fry

INGREDIENTS:

- 1 lb beef sirloin, sliced thin
- 1 red bell pepper, sliced
- 1 zucchini, sliced
- 1 small onion, sliced
- 2 tbsp coconut aminos (or soy sauce alternative)
- 1 tbsp sesame oil
- 1 tsp garlic powder
- 1 tsp ginger powder
- 1/2 tsp chili flakes (optional)
- Salt and pepper to taste
- Cooking spray or olive oil

Prep Time: 10 min   **Cook Time: 12 min**   **ᴹServes: 4**

DIRECTIONS:

1. Preheat the air fryer to 375°F (190°C). **2.** In a bowl, combine coconut aminos, sesame oil, garlic powder, ginger powder, chili flakes, salt, and pepper. **3.** Toss the sliced beef and vegetables in the marinade. **4.** Lightly spray the air fryer basket with cooking spray. **5.** Place the beef and vegetables in a single layer in the air fryer basket. **6.** Cook for 10-12 minutes, shaking the basket halfway through, until the beef is fully cooked and the vegetables are tender.

NUTRITIONAL INFORMATION

Per serving: 280 calories, 22g protein, 5g carbohydrates, 18g fat, 1g fiber, 65mg cholesterol, 400mg sodium, 400mg potassium.

Balsamic-Glazed Pork Loin

INGREDIENTS:

- 1 lb pork loin
- 2 tbsp balsamic vinegar (sugar-free)
- 1 tbsp olive oil
- 1 tbsp Dijon mustard
- 1 tsp garlic powder
- 1 tsp dried thyme
- Salt and pepper to taste
- Cooking spray or olive oil

Prep Time: 10 min   **Cook Time: 20 min**   **Serves: 4**

DIRECTIONS:

1. In a small bowl, mix balsamic vinegar, olive oil, Dijon mustard, garlic powder, thyme, salt, and pepper. **2.** Rub the balsamic mixture evenly over the pork loin. Let marinate for at least 10 minutes. **3.** Preheat the air fryer to 375°F (190°C). **4.** Lightly spray the air fryer basket with cooking spray. **5.** Place the pork loin in the basket and cook for 18-20 minutes, flipping halfway through, until the internal temperature reaches 145°F. **6.** Let the pork rest for 5 minutes before slicing.

NUTRITIONAL INFORMATION

Per serving: 290 calories, 26g protein, 2g carbohydrates, 19g fat, 0g fiber, 80mg cholesterol, 350mg sodium, 400mg potassium.

Moroccan Lamb Ribs

INGREDIENTS:

- 1 lb lamb ribs
- 2 tbsp olive oil
- 1 tsp ground cumin
- 1 tsp ground coriander
- 1 tsp paprika
- 1/2 tsp ground cinnamon
- 1/2 tsp garlic powder
- 1/4 tsp cayenne pepper (optional)
- Salt and pepper to taste
- Cooking spray or olive oil

Prep Time: 10 min   **Cook Time: 25 min**   **Serves: 4**

DIRECTIONS:

1. In a small bowl, mix olive oil, cumin, coriander, paprika, cinnamon, garlic powder, cayenne pepper, salt, and pepper. **2.** Rub the spice mixture evenly over the lamb ribs. Let the ribs marinate for 15 minutes if desired. **3.** Preheat the air fryer to 375°F (190°C). **4.** Lightly spray the air fryer basket with cooking spray. **5.** Place the lamb ribs in the basket in a single layer. **6.** Cook for 20-25 minutes, flipping halfway through, until the ribs are crispy and fully cooked (internal temperature of 145°F).

NUTRITIONAL INFORMATION

Per serving: 400 calories, 25g protein, 2g carbohydrates, 32g fat, 0g fiber, 90mg cholesterol, 400mg sodium, 350mg potassium.

BBQ Pulled Pork

INGREDIENTS:

- 1.5 lbs pork shoulder or pork butt, cut into 2-3 inch pieces
- 1 tbsp olive oil
- 1 tsp smoked paprika
- 1 tsp garlic powder
- 1/2 tsp onion powder
- 1/2 tsp cumin
- Salt and pepper to taste
- 1/4 cup sugar-free BBQ sauce
- Cooking spray or olive oil

Prep Time: 10 min   **Cook Time: 30 min**   **Serves: 4**

DIRECTIONS:

1. In a bowl, mix olive oil, smoked paprika, garlic powder, onion powder, cumin, salt, and pepper. **2.** Rub the spice mixture over the pork pieces and let marinate for 10 minutes. **3.** Preheat the air fryer to 350°F (175°C). **4.** Lightly spray the air fryer basket with cooking spray or olive oil. **5.** Place pork pieces in the basket and cook for 25-30 minutes, flipping halfway through, until pork is tender and cooked through (internal temperature should reach 190°F). **6.** Shred the pork using two forks, then toss with sugar-free BBQ sauce.

NUTRITIONAL INFORMATION

Per serving: 350 calories, 28g protein, 3g carbohydrates, 25g fat, 0g fiber, 90mg cholesterol, 450mg sodium, 400mg potassium.

Italian-Style Meatballs

INGREDIENTS:

- 1 lb ground beef (or ground pork)
- 1/4 cup almond flour
- 1/4 cup grated Parmesan cheese
- 1 large egg
- 2 cloves garlic, minced
- 1 tsp dried Italian seasoning
- 1/2 tsp onion powder
- Salt and pepper to taste
- Cooking spray or olive oil

Prep Time: 10 min   **Cook Time: 12 min**   **Serves: 4**

DIRECTIONS:

1. In a large bowl, combine the ground meat, almond flour, Parmesan, egg, garlic, Italian seasoning, onion powder, salt, and pepper. Mix until well combined. **2.** Form the mixture into 12 evenly sized meatballs. **3.** Preheat the air fryer to 375°F (190°C). **4.** Lightly spray the air fryer basket with cooking spray or olive oil. **5.** Place the meatballs in a single layer in the basket. **6.** Cook for 10-12 minutes, shaking the basket halfway through, until the meatballs are browned and reach an internal temperature of 160°F.

NUTRITIONAL INFORMATION

Per serving: 280 calories, 22g protein, 3g carbohydrates, 19g fat, 1g fiber, 90mg cholesterol, 450mg sodium, 300mg potassium.

Crispy Pork Belly

INGREDIENTS:

- 1 lb pork belly, cut into 1-inch cubes
- 1 tbsp olive oil
- 1 tsp garlic powder
- 1 tsp smoked paprika
- Salt and pepper to taste
- Cooking spray or olive oil

Prep Time: 10 min   **Cook Time: 25 min**   **Serves: 4**

DIRECTIONS:

1. Preheat the air fryer to 375°F (190°C). **2.** In a bowl, toss the pork belly cubes with olive oil, garlic powder, smoked paprika, salt, and pepper. **3.** Lightly spray the air fryer basket with cooking spray or oil. **4.** Place the pork belly cubes in a single layer in the air fryer basket. **5.** Cook for 20-25 minutes, shaking the basket halfway through, until the pork belly is crispy and golden on the outside. **6.** Let the pork belly rest for a few minutes before serving.

NUTRITIONAL INFORMATION

Per serving: 350 calories, 20g protein, 1g carbohydrates, 30g fat, 0g fiber, 60mg cholesterol, 400mg sodium, 300mg potassium.

Beef and Broccoli Stir-Fry

INGREDIENTS:

- 1 lb beef sirloin, thinly sliced
- 2 cups broccoli florets
- 2 tbsp coconut aminos (or soy sauce alternative)
- 1 tbsp sesame oil
- 1 tsp garlic powder
- 1 tsp ginger powder
- Salt and pepper to taste
- Cooking spray or olive oil

Prep Time: 10 min   **Cook Time: 15 min**   **Serves: 4**

DIRECTIONS:

1. Preheat the air fryer to 375°F (190°C). **2.** In a bowl, mix coconut aminos, sesame oil, garlic powder, ginger powder, salt, and pepper. **3.** Toss the sliced beef and broccoli florets in the marinade until evenly coated. **4.** Lightly spray the air fryer basket with cooking spray or olive oil. **5.** Place the beef and broccoli in a single layer in the air fryer basket. **6.** Cook for 12-15 minutes, shaking the basket halfway through to ensure even cooking, until the beef is cooked and the broccoli is tender.

NUTRITIONAL INFORMATION

Per serving: 280 calories, 22g protein, 5g carbohydrates, 18g fat, 2g fiber, 70mg cholesterol, 400mg sodium, 350mg potassium.

Air-Fried Brisket with Garlic Butter

INGREDIENTS:

- 1.5 lbs beef brisket
- 2 tbsp olive oil
- 1 tsp smoked paprika
- 1 tsp garlic powder
- 1 tsp onion powder
- Salt and pepper to taste
- 2 tbsp butter, melted
- 3 cloves garlic, minced
- 1 tbsp fresh parsley, chopped (optional)

 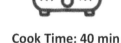

Prep Time: 10 min   **Cook Time: 40 min**   **Serves: 4**

DIRECTIONS:

1. Preheat the air fryer to 350°F (175°C). **2.** Rub the brisket with olive oil, smoked paprika, garlic powder, onion powder, salt, and pepper. **3.** Place the brisket in the air fryer basket and cook for 35-40 minutes, flipping halfway through. Ensure the internal temperature reaches 195°F for tender meat. **4.** While the brisket is cooking, mix melted butter with minced garlic and parsley. **5.** After cooking, let the brisket rest for 10 minutes, then slice it and drizzle with garlic butter sauce.

NUTRITIONAL INFORMATION

Per serving: 400 calories, 28g protein, 2g carbohydrates, 30g fat, 0g fiber, 90mg cholesterol, 400mg sodium, 350mg potassium.

Stuffed Bell Peppers with Ground Beef

INGREDIENTS:

- 3 large bell peppers, halved and seeded
- 250g ground beef
- 1/2 cup chopped spinach
- 1/4 cup shredded mozzarella cheese
- 2 tbsp tomato paste (no sugar added)
- 1 tbsp olive oil
- 1/2 tsp garlic powder
- 1/4 tsp salt
- 1/4 tsp black pepper

Prep Time: 10 min   **Cook Time: 15 min**   **Serves: 3**

DIRECTIONS:

1. Preheat the air fryer to 360°F (180°C). **2.** Sauté ground beef with olive oil, garlic powder, salt, and pepper in a pan. **3.** Mix in spinach and tomato paste, cooking until well combined. **4.** Fill bell pepper halves with the beef mixture, top with cheese. **5.** Cook peppers in the air fryer at 360°F (180°C) for 12-15 minutes.

Serving Suggestion: Serve with a side of mixed greens or avocado.

NUTRITIONAL INFORMATION

290 calories, 22g protein, 6g carbohydrates, 20g fat, 2g fiber, 50mg cholesterol, 350mg sodium, 450mg potassium.

Pork Tenderloin with Dijon Cream Sauce

INGREDIENTS:

- 1 lb (450g) pork tenderloin
- 1 tbsp olive oil
- 1/2 tsp garlic powder
- 1/2 tsp salt
- 1/4 tsp black pepper
- 1/4 cup heavy cream
- 1 tbsp Dijon mustard
- 1/2 tsp lemon juice
- Optional: 1 tsp chopped fresh parsley

Prep Time: 5 min   **Cook Time: 18 min**   **Serves: 4**

DIRECTIONS:

1. Preheat the air fryer to 400°F (200°C). **2.** Rub pork with olive oil, garlic powder, salt, and pepper. **3.** Cook in the air fryer at 400°F (200°C) for 15-18 minutes, flipping halfway. **4.** Mix heavy cream, Dijon mustard, and lemon juice; heat until warm. **5.** Let pork rest for 5 minutes before slicing and topping with sauce.

Serving Suggestion: Serve with steamed asparagus or cauliflower mash.

NUTRITIONAL INFORMATION

290 calories, 24g protein, 2g carbohydrates, 21g fat, 0g fiber, 80mg cholesterol, 320mg sodium, 350mg potassium.

Garlic Butter Shrimp

INGREDIENTS:

- 1 lb large shrimp, peeled and deveined
- 2 tbsp melted butter
- 3 cloves garlic, minced
- 1 tbsp olive oil
- 1 tsp paprika
- 1/2 tsp garlic powder
- Salt and pepper to taste
- 1 tbsp fresh parsley, chopped (optional)
- Lemon wedges for serving

Prep Time: 5 min **Cook Time: 10 min** **Serves: 4**

DIRECTIONS:

1. Preheat the air fryer to 400°F (200°C). **2.** In a bowl, mix melted butter, olive oil, minced garlic, paprika, garlic powder, salt, and pepper. **3.** Toss the shrimp in the garlic butter mixture until evenly coated. **4.** Lightly spray the air fryer basket with cooking spray or olive oil. **5.** Place the shrimp in a single layer in the basket. **6.** Cook for 8-10 minutes, shaking the basket halfway through, until the shrimp are pink and cooked through. **7.** Garnish with fresh parsley and serve with lemon wedges.

NUTRITIONAL INFORMATION

Per serving: 220 calories, 24g protein, 1g carbohydrates, 14g fat, 0g fiber, 195mg cholesterol, 400mg sodium, 200mg potassium.

Keto Salmon with Lemon and Dill

INGREDIENTS:

- 4 salmon fillets (6 oz each)
- 2 tbsp olive oil
- 1 tbsp fresh lemon juice
- 1 tsp lemon zest
- 1 tbsp fresh dill, chopped (or 1 tsp dried dill)
- 2 cloves garlic, minced
- Salt and pepper to taste
- Lemon wedges for serving

Prep Time: 5 min **Cook Time: 10 min** **Serves: 4**

DIRECTIONS:

1. Preheat the air fryer to 400°F (200°C). **2.** In a small bowl, mix olive oil, lemon juice, lemon zest, dill, minced garlic, salt, and pepper. **3.** Brush the salmon fillets with the lemon and dill mixture on both sides. **4.** Lightly spray the air fryer basket with cooking spray or olive oil. **5.** Place the salmon fillets skin-side down in the basket. **6.** Cook for 8-10 minutes, depending on the thickness of the fillets, until the salmon is flaky and cooked through. **7.** Serve with lemon wedges for extra flavor.

NUTRITIONAL INFORMATION

Per serving: 310 calories, 28g protein, 1g carbohydrates, 21g fat, 0g fiber, 70mg cholesterol, 350mg sodium, 400mg potassium.

Parmesan-Crusted Cod

INGREDIENTS:

- 4 cod fillets (6 oz each)
- 1/2 cup grated Parmesan cheese
- 1/4 cup almond flour
- 1 tsp garlic powder
- 1 tsp paprika
- 1 large egg, beaten
- Salt and pepper to taste
- Lemon wedges for serving
- Cooking spray or olive oil

Prep Time: 5 min   **Cook Time: 12 min**   **Serves: 4**

DIRECTIONS:

1. Preheat the air fryer to 400°F (200°C). **2.** In one bowl, whisk the egg. In another bowl, mix Parmesan, almond flour, garlic powder, paprika, salt, and pepper. **3.** Dip each cod fillet in the beaten egg, then coat with the Parmesan mixture. **4.** Lightly spray the air fryer basket with cooking spray or olive oil. **5.** Place the fillets in a single layer in the air fryer basket. **6.** Cook for 10-12 minutes, flipping halfway through, until golden and the fish flakes easily with a fork. **7.** Serve with lemon wedges for added flavor.

NUTRITIONAL INFORMATION

Per serving: 280 calories, 35g protein, 3g carbohydrates, 15g fat, 1g fiber, 70mg cholesterol, 350mg sodium, 400mg potassium.

Crispy Tuna Cakes

INGREDIENTS:

- 2 cans tuna (5 oz each), drained
- 1/4 cup almond flour
- 1 large egg
- 1/4 cup grated Parmesan cheese
- 1 tbsp mayonnaise (sugar-free)
- 1 tsp Dijon mustard
- 1 tsp garlic powder
- 1 tsp onion powder
- 1 tbsp fresh parsley, chopped (optional)
- Salt and pepper to taste
- Cooking spray or olive oil

Prep Time: 10 min   **Cook Time: 12 min**   **Serves: 4**

DIRECTIONS:

1. In a bowl, combine drained tuna, almond flour, egg, Parmesan, mayonnaise, Dijon mustard, garlic powder, onion powder, parsley, salt, and pepper. Mix well. **2.** Form the mixture into 6 small patties. **3.** Preheat the air fryer to 375°F (190°C). **4.** Lightly spray the air fryer basket with cooking spray or olive oil. **5.** Place the tuna cakes in a single layer in the basket. **6.** Air fry for 10-12 minutes, flipping halfway through, until the cakes are golden brown and crispy.

NUTRITIONAL INFORMATION

Per serving: 230 calories, 22g protein, 3g carbohydrates, 14g fat, 1g fiber, 80mg cholesterol, 450mg sodium, 300mg potassium.

Cajun-Spiced Catfish

INGREDIENTS:
- 4 catfish fillets (about 6 oz each)
- 2 tbsp olive oil
- 1 tbsp Cajun seasoning
- 1/2 tsp garlic powder
- 1/2 tsp smoked paprika
- Salt and pepper to taste
- Lemon wedges for serving
- Cooking spray or olive oil

Prep Time: 5 min   **Cook Time: 12 min**   **мServes: 4**

DIRECTIONS:

1. Preheat the air fryer to 400°F (200°C). **2.** In a small bowl, mix olive oil, Cajun seasoning, garlic powder, smoked paprika, salt, and pepper. **3.** Rub the catfish fillets with the seasoning mixture, ensuring an even coat. **4.** Lightly spray the air fryer basket with cooking spray or olive oil. **5.** Place the catfish fillets in a single layer in the air fryer basket. **6.** Air fry for 10-12 minutes, flipping halfway through, until the fish is cooked through and flakes easily with a fork. **7.** Serve with lemon wedges for added flavor.

NUTRITIONAL INFORMATION

Per serving: 280 calories, 28g protein, 2g carbohydrates, 18g fat, 0g fiber, 80mg cholesterol, 450mg sodium, 400mg potassium.

Shrimp Scampi

INGREDIENTS:
- 1 lb large shrimp, peeled and deveined
- 2 tbsp butter, melted
- 2 tbsp olive oil
- 4 cloves garlic, minced
- 1 tbsp fresh lemon juice
- 1 tsp lemon zest
- 1/2 tsp red pepper flakes (optional)
- 1 tbsp fresh parsley, chopped
- Salt and pepper to taste
- Lemon wedges for serving

Prep Time: 5 min   **Cook Time: 10 min**   **Serves: 4**

DIRECTIONS:

1. Preheat the air fryer to 400°F (200°C). **2.** In a bowl, mix melted butter, olive oil, garlic, lemon juice, lemon zest, red pepper flakes, salt, and pepper. **3.** Toss the shrimp in the garlic butter mixture until well coated. **4.** Place the shrimp in a single layer in the air fryer basket. **5.** Cook for 8-10 minutes, shaking the basket halfway through, until the shrimp are pink and cooked through. **6.** Garnish with fresh parsley and serve with lemon wedges.

NUTRITIONAL INFORMATION

Per serving: 250 calories, 24g protein, 2g carbohydrates, 18g fat, 0g fiber, 200mg cholesterol, 450mg sodium, 200mg potassium.

Coconut Shrimp with Spicy Mayo

INGREDIENTS:

- **For the Shrimp:**
- 1 lb large shrimp, peeled and deveined
- 1/2 cup unsweetened shredded coconut
- 1/4 cup almond flour
- 1/4 tsp garlic powder
- 1/4 tsp paprika
- 1 large egg, beaten
- Salt and pepper to taste
- Cooking spray or olive oil
- **For the Spicy Mayo:**
- 1/4 cup mayonnaise (sugar-free)
- 1 tsp Sriracha (adjust to spice preference)
- 1 tsp lime juice

мPrep Time: 10 min   Cook Time: 10 min   Serves: 4

DIRECTIONS:

1. Preheat the air fryer to 375°F (190°C). **2.** In one bowl, whisk the egg. In another bowl, combine shredded coconut, almond flour, garlic powder, paprika, salt, and pepper. **3.** Dip each shrimp in the beaten egg, then coat in the coconut mixture. **4.** Lightly spray the air fryer basket with cooking spray or olive oil. **5.** Place the shrimp in a single layer in the basket. **6.** Cook for 8-10 minutes, flipping halfway through, until golden and crispy. **For the Spicy Mayo:** In a small bowl, mix mayonnaise, Sriracha, and lime juice. Stir until smooth.

NUTRITIONAL INFORMATION

Per serving: 290 calories, 23g protein, 3g carbohydrates, 20g fat, 1g fiber, 200mg cholesterol, 450mg sodium, 200mg potassium.

Air-Fried Fish Tacos with Avocado Crema

INGREDIENTS:

- **For the Fish:**
- 1 lb white fish fillets (cod, tilapia, or haddock)
- 1/2 cup almond flour
- 1/4 cup grated Parmesan cheese
- 1 tsp smoked paprika
- 1/2 tsp garlic powder
- 1 large egg, beaten
- Salt and pepper to taste
- Low-carb tortillas (optional)
- Cooking spray or olive oil
- **For the Avocado Crema:**
- 1 ripe avocado
- 1/4 cup sour cream
- 1 tbsp lime juice
- 1/4 tsp garlic powder
- Salt and pepper to taste

Prep Time: 10 min   Cook Time: 12 min   Serves: 4

DIRECTIONS:

1. Preheat the air fryer to 375°F (190°C). **2.** In one bowl, whisk the egg. In another bowl, combine almond flour, Parmesan, smoked paprika, garlic powder, salt, and pepper. **3.** Dip each fish fillet in the egg, then coat with the almond flour mixture. **4.** Lightly spray the air fryer basket with cooking spray or olive oil. **5.** Place fish fillets in a single layer in the air fryer basket and cook for 10-12 minutes, flipping halfway through, until golden and cooked through. **For the Avocado Crema:** In a bowl, mash the avocado and mix with sour cream, lime juice, garlic powder, salt, and pepper until smooth.

NUTRITIONAL INFORMATION

Per serving: 320 calories, 28g protein, 5g carbohydrates, 20g fat, 3g fiber, 70mg cholesterol, 450mg sodium, 400mg potassium.

Keto Crab Cakes

INGREDIENTS:

- 1 lb lump crab meat
- 1/4 cup almond flour
- 1 large egg
- 2 tbsp mayonnaise (sugar-free)
- 1 tbsp Dijon mustard
- 1 tsp Old Bay seasoning
- 1/2 tsp garlic powder
- 1 tsp fresh lemon juice
- 1 tbsp fresh parsley, chopped (optional)
- Salt and pepper to taste
- Cooking spray or olive oil

Prep Time: 10 min   **Cook Time: 12 min**   **Serves: 4**

DIRECTIONS:

1. In a large bowl, combine crab meat, almond flour, egg, mayonnaise, Dijon mustard, Old Bay seasoning, garlic powder, lemon juice, parsley, salt, and pepper. Mix gently until combined. **2.** Form the mixture into 8 small patties. **3.** Preheat the air fryer to 375°F (190°C). **4.** Lightly spray the air fryer basket with cooking spray or olive oil. **5.** Place the crab cakes in a single layer in the basket. **6.** Air fry for 10-12 minutes, flipping halfway through, until golden brown and crispy.

NUTRITIONAL INFORMATION

Per serving: 220 calories, 23g protein, 3g carbohydrates, 12g fat, 1g fiber, 80mg cholesterol, 450mg sodium, 300mg potassium.

Garlic Butter Lobster Tails

INGREDIENTS:

- 2 lobster tails (about 5-6 oz each)
- 2 tbsp butter, melted
- 2 cloves garlic, minced
- 1 tsp fresh lemon juice
- 1 tsp fresh parsley, chopped (optional)
- Salt and pepper to taste
- Cooking spray or olive oil

Prep Time: 5 min   **Cook Time: 10 min**   **Serves: 2**

DIRECTIONS:

1. Preheat the air fryer to 380°F (190°C). **2.** Using kitchen shears, carefully cut through the top of the lobster shell down to the tail, exposing the lobster meat. Gently lift the meat out of the shell, keeping it attached at the base. **3.** In a small bowl, mix melted butter, garlic, lemon juice, parsley, salt, and pepper. **4.** Brush the lobster meat generously with the garlic butter mixture. **5.** Lightly spray the air fryer basket with cooking spray or olive oil. **6.** Place the lobster tails in the air fryer basket, shell side down. **7.** Cook for 8-10 minutes, until the lobster meat is opaque and cooked through.

NUTRITIONAL INFORMATION

Per serving: 240 calories, 22g protein, 1g carbohydrates, 17g fat, 0g fiber, 140mg cholesterol, 350mg sodium, 150mg potassium.

Blackened Tilapia

Prep Time: 5 min   **Cook Time: 12 min**   **Serves: 4**

INGREDIENTS:

- 4 tilapia fillets (about 6 oz each)
- 2 tbsp olive oil
- 1 tbsp smoked paprika
- 1 tsp garlic powder
- 1 tsp onion powder
- 1/2 tsp cayenne pepper (optional for extra heat)
- 1/2 tsp dried thyme
- 1/2 tsp dried oregano
- Salt and pepper to taste
- Lemon wedges for serving
- Cooking spray or olive oil

DIRECTIONS:

1. Preheat the air fryer to 400°F (200°C). **2.** In a small bowl, mix olive oil, smoked paprika, garlic powder, onion powder, cayenne pepper, thyme, oregano, salt, and pepper. **3.** Brush the tilapia fillets with the olive oil mixture, coating both sides evenly. **4.** Lightly spray the air fryer basket with cooking spray or olive oil. **5.** Place the tilapia fillets in a single layer in the air fryer basket. **6.** Cook for 10-12 minutes, flipping halfway through, until the fish is cooked through and flaky. **7.** Serve with lemon wedges for extra flavor.

NUTRITIONAL INFORMATION

Per serving: 230 calories, 25g protein, 2g carbohydrates, 13g fat, 0g fiber, 70mg cholesterol, 400mg sodium, 350mg potassium.

Lemon Pepper Salmon

Prep Time: 5 min   **Cook Time: 10 min**   **Serves: 4**

INGREDIENTS:

- 4 salmon fillets (6 oz each)
- 2 tbsp olive oil
- 1 tbsp fresh lemon juice
- 1 tsp lemon zest
- 1 tsp garlic powder
- 1 tsp freshly ground black pepper
- 1/2 tsp salt
- Lemon wedges for serving
- Cooking spray or olive oil

DIRECTIONS:

1. Preheat the air fryer to 400°F (200°C). **2.** In a small bowl, mix olive oil, lemon juice, lemon zest, garlic powder, black pepper, and salt. **3.** Brush the salmon fillets with the lemon pepper mixture, coating both sides evenly. **4.** Lightly spray the air fryer basket with cooking spray or olive oil. **5.** Place the salmon fillets skin-side down in the air fryer basket. **6.** Cook for 8-10 minutes, depending on the thickness of the fillets, until the salmon is flaky and cooked through. **7.** Serve with lemon wedges for added flavor.

NUTRITIONAL INFORMATION

Per serving: 320 calories, 28g protein, 1g carbohydrates, 22g fat, 0g fiber, 70mg cholesterol, 350mg sodium, 400mg potassium.

Scallops with Garlic Butter Sauce

INGREDIENTS:

- 1 lb large sea scallops
- 2 tbsp olive oil
- Salt and pepper to taste
- 2 tbsp butter, melted
- 3 cloves garlic, minced
- 1 tbsp fresh lemon juice
- 1 tbsp fresh parsley, chopped (optional)

Prep Time: 5 min **Cook Time: 8 min** мServes: 4

DIRECTIONS:

1. Preheat the air fryer to 400°F (200°C). **2.** Pat the scallops dry with a paper towel, then drizzle with olive oil and season with salt and pepper. **3.** Lightly spray the air fryer basket with cooking spray or olive oil. **4.** Place the scallops in a single layer in the air fryer basket. **5.** Cook for 6-8 minutes, flipping halfway through, until the scallops are firm and golden. **6.** In a small saucepan, melt the butter over medium heat. Add minced garlic and sauté for 1-2 minutes. Stir in lemon juice and parsley. **7.** Drizzle the garlic butter sauce over the cooked scallops before serving.

NUTRITIONAL INFORMATION

Per serving: 230 calories, 22g protein, 1g carbohydrates, 16g fat, 0g fiber, 60mg cholesterol, 400mg sodium, 300mg potassium.

Air-Fried Calamari

INGREDIENTS:

- 1 lb calamari rings (squid), cleaned
- 1/2 cup almond flour
- 1/4 cup grated Parmesan cheese
- 1 tsp smoked paprika
- 1/2 tsp garlic powder
- 1/2 tsp onion powder
- 1 large egg, beaten
- Salt and pepper to taste
- Lemon wedges for serving
- Cooking spray or olive oil

Prep Time: 10 min **Cook Time: 10 min** **Serves: 4**

DIRECTIONS:

1. Preheat the air fryer to 400°F (200°C). **2.** In a bowl, whisk the egg. In a separate bowl, combine almond flour, Parmesan cheese, smoked paprika, garlic powder, onion powder, salt, and pepper. **3.** Dip each calamari ring into the beaten egg, then coat with the almond flour mixture. **4.** Lightly spray the air fryer basket with cooking spray or olive oil. **5.** Place the calamari rings in a single layer in the basket. **6.** Air fry for 8-10 minutes, shaking the basket halfway through, until the calamari is golden and crispy.

NUTRITIONAL INFORMATION

Per serving: 230 calories, 20g protein, 3g carbohydrates, 14g fat, 1g fiber, 200mg cholesterol, 450mg sodium, 300mg potassium.

Spicy Salmon Skewers

INGREDIENTS:

- 1 lb salmon fillets, cut into 1-inch cubes
- 2 tbsp olive oil
- 1 tbsp Sriracha (or your preferred hot sauce)
- 1 tsp garlic powder
- 1 tsp paprika
- 1/2 tsp cayenne pepper (optional for extra heat)
- 1 tsp lemon juice
- Salt and pepper to taste
- Wooden skewers (soaked in water for 30 minutes)

Prep Time: 10 min   **Cook Time: 10 min**   **Serves: 4**

DIRECTIONS:

1. Preheat the air fryer to 375°F (190°C). **2.** In a bowl, mix olive oil, Sriracha, garlic powder, paprika, cayenne pepper, lemon juice, salt, and pepper. **3.** Toss the salmon cubes in the spicy mixture until evenly coated. **4.** Thread the salmon cubes onto the soaked skewers. **5.** Lightly spray the air fryer basket with cooking spray or olive oil. **6.** Place the skewers in the air fryer basket and cook for 8-10 minutes, flipping halfway through, until the salmon is cooked through and slightly charred.

NUTRITIONAL INFORMATION

Per serving: 320 calories, 28g protein, 2g carbohydrates, 22g fat, 0g fiber, 70mg cholesterol, 350mg sodium, 400mg potassium.

Keto Coconut-Crusted Salmon

INGREDIENTS:

- 4 salmon fillets (6 oz each)
- 1/2 cup unsweetened shredded coconut
- 1/4 cup almond flour
- 1 large egg, beaten
- 1 tbsp coconut oil, melted
- 1 tsp garlic powder
- 1 tsp paprika
- Salt and pepper to taste
- Cooking spray or olive oil

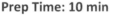

Prep Time: 10 min   **Cook Time: 10 min**   **Serves: 4**

DIRECTIONS:

1. Preheat the air fryer to 375°F (190°C). **2.** In one bowl, whisk the egg. In another bowl, mix the shredded coconut, almond flour, garlic powder, paprika, salt, and pepper. **3.** Brush the salmon fillets with melted coconut oil, then dip each fillet into the beaten egg and coat with the coconut-almond mixture. **4.** Lightly spray the air fryer basket with cooking spray or olive oil. **5.** Place the salmon fillets in a single layer in the air fryer basket. **6.** Cook for 8-10 minutes, flipping halfway through, until the salmon is crispy and cooked through.

NUTRITIONAL INFORMATION

Per serving: 350 calories, 28g protein, 4g carbohydrates, 25g fat, 2g fiber, 70mg cholesterol, 350mg sodium, 400mg potassium.

Air-Fried Garlic Parmesan Shrimp

INGREDIENTS:

- 1 lb (450g) large shrimp, peeled and deveined
- 2 tbsp olive oil
- 1/4 cup grated Parmesan cheese
- 2 cloves garlic, minced
- 1/2 tsp paprika
- 1/4 tsp salt
- 1/4 tsp black pepper
- Optional: 1 tbsp chopped fresh parsley

Prep Time: 5min   **Cook Time: 8 min**   **Serves: 4**

DIRECTIONS:

1. Preheat the air fryer to 400°F (200°C). **2.** Toss shrimp with olive oil, Parmesan, garlic, paprika, salt, and pepper. **3.** Arrange shrimp in a single layer in the air fryer basket. **4.** Cook at 400°F (200°C) for 6-8 minutes, shaking the basket halfway through.
Serving Suggestion: Serve with a side of zucchini noodles or a fresh salad.

NUTRITIONAL INFORMATION

220 calories, 23g protein, 2g carbohydrates, 14g fat, 0g fiber, 175mg cholesterol, 480mg sodium, 280mg potassium.

Lemon Herb Mahi-Mahi

INGREDIENTS:

- 4 Mahi-Mahi fillets (about 6 oz each)
- 2 tbsp olive oil
- 2 tbsp lemon juice
- 1 tsp dried oregano
- 1 tsp dried thyme
- 1/2 tsp garlic powder
- 1/4 tsp salt
- 1/4 tsp black pepper
- Optional: lemon slices for garnish

Prep Time: 5 min   **Cook Time: 10 min**   **Serves: 4**

DIRECTIONS:

1. Preheat the air fryer to 380°F (190°C). **2.** Mix olive oil, lemon juice, oregano, thyme, garlic powder, salt, and pepper. **3.** Coat Mahi-Mahi fillets with the mixture. **4.** Place fillets in the air fryer basket in a single layer. **5.** Cook at 380°F (190°C) for 8-10 minutes, flipping halfway.
Serving Suggestion: Serve with a side of steamed asparagus or a mixed green salad.

NUTRITIONAL INFORMATION

220 calories, 28g protein, 1g carbohydrates, 11g fat, 0g fiber, 80mg cholesterol, 320mg sodium, 420mg potassium.

Keto Tuna Salad Stuffed Avocados

INGREDIENTS:

- 2 ripe avocados, halved and pitted
- 1 can (5 oz) tuna in water, drained
- 2 tbsp mayonnaise
- 1 tbsp olive oil
- 1 tbsp lemon juice
- 1/4 tsp garlic powder
- 1/4 tsp salt
- 1/4 tsp black pepper
- Optional: 1 tbsp chopped celery or red onion

мPrep Time: 5 min   Cook Time: 5 min   Serves: 4

DIRECTIONS:

1. Mix tuna, mayonnaise, olive oil, lemon juice, garlic powder, salt, and optional ingredients. **2.** Spoon tuna salad into avocado halves. **3.** If desired, warm avocados in the air fryer at 350°F (180°C) for 3-5 minutes.

Serving Suggestion: Serve chilled or slightly warm with fresh herbs.

NUTRITIONAL INFORMATION

240 calories, 12g protein, 6g carbohydrates, 20g fat, 5g fiber, 15mg cholesterol, 320mg sodium, 480mg potassium.

Crispy Air-Fried Salmon Bites

INGREDIENTS:

- 1 lb (450g) salmon fillet, cut into 1-inch cubes
- 2 tbsp olive oil
- 1/4 cup almond flour
- 1/4 cup grated Parmesan cheese
- 1/2 tsp garlic powder
- 1/2 tsp paprika
- 1/4 tsp salt
- 1/4 tsp black pepper
- Optional: 1 tsp lemon zest

Prep Time: 5 min   Cook Time: 10 min   Serves: 4

DIRECTIONS:

1. Preheat the air fryer to 400°F (200°C). **2.** Toss salmon cubes with olive oil, then coat with almond flour, Parmesan, garlic powder, paprika, salt, pepper, and optional lemon zest. **3.** Place salmon bites in the air fryer basket in a single layer. **4.** Cook at 400°F (200°C) for 8-10 minutes, shaking the basket halfway through.

Serving Suggestion: Serve with a side of lemon wedges or a low-carb dipping sauce.

NUTRITIONAL INFORMATION

320 calories, 25g protein, 3g carbohydrates, 23g fat, 1g fiber, 65mg cholesterol, 320mg sodium, 350mg potassium.

Cheesy Cauliflower Mash

INGREDIENTS:

- 1 large head of cauliflower, chopped into florets
- 1/2 cup shredded cheddar cheese
- 1/4 cup cream cheese, softened
- 2 tbsp butter
- 1/4 tsp garlic powder
- Salt and pepper to taste
- 1 tbsp fresh chives, chopped (optional)

Prep Time: 10 min   **Cook Time: 15 min**   **Serves: 4**

DIRECTIONS:

1. Preheat the air fryer to 375°F (190°C). **2.** Place the cauliflower florets in a microwave-safe dish with a tablespoon of water and cover. Microwave for 5-7 minutes until tender. **3.** Transfer the cooked cauliflower to a food processor or blender. Add the butter, cream cheese, garlic powder, salt, and pepper. Blend until smooth. **4.** Stir in the shredded cheddar cheese. **5.** Transfer the cauliflower mash into a small oven-safe dish or ramekin. **6.** Air fry for 5-7 minutes until the cheese is melted and the top is slightly golden. **7.** Garnish with fresh chives before serving.

NUTRITIONAL INFORMATION

Per serving: 180 calories, 6g protein, 6g carbohydrates, 14g fat, 2g fiber, 35mg cholesterol, 200mg sodium, 300mg potassium.

Garlic Parmesan Brussels Sprouts

INGREDIENTS:

- 1 lb Brussels sprouts, halved
- 2 tbsp olive oil
- 1/4 cup grated Parmesan cheese
- 2 cloves garlic, minced
- 1/2 tsp garlic powder
- Salt and pepper to taste
- 1 tbsp fresh parsley, chopped (optional)
- Cooking spray or olive oil

Prep Time: 10 min   **Cook Time: 15 min**   **Serves: 4**

DIRECTIONS:

1. Preheat the air fryer to 375°F (190°C). **2.** In a large bowl, toss the halved Brussels sprouts with olive oil, minced garlic, garlic powder, salt, and pepper. **3.** Lightly spray the air fryer basket with cooking spray or olive oil. **4.** Place the Brussels sprouts in a single layer in the air fryer basket. **5.** Air fry for 12-15 minutes, shaking the basket halfway through, until the Brussels sprouts are crispy and golden brown. **6.** Once cooked, transfer the Brussels sprouts to a bowl and toss with Parmesan cheese. **7.** Garnish with fresh parsley before serving.

NUTRITIONAL INFORMATION

Per serving: 140 calories, 5g protein, 8g carbohydrates, 10g fat, 4g fiber, 5mg cholesterol, 200mg sodium, 400mg potassium.

Air-Fried Green Beans with Bacon

INGREDIENTS:

- 1 lb fresh green beans, trimmed
- 4 slices of bacon, chopped
- 1 tbsp olive oil
- 2 cloves garlic, minced
- Salt and pepper to taste
- 1/4 tsp smoked paprika (optional)
- Cooking spray or olive oil

Prep Time: 10 min   **Cook Time: 12 min**   **Serves: 4**

DIRECTIONS:

1. Preheat the air fryer to 375°F (190°C). **2.** In a bowl, toss the green beans with olive oil, garlic, salt, pepper, and smoked paprika (if using). **3.** Lightly spray the air fryer basket with cooking spray or olive oil. **4.** Spread the chopped bacon evenly over the green beans. **5.** Place the green beans and bacon mixture in a single layer in the air fryer basket. **6.** Air fry for 10-12 minutes, shaking the basket halfway through, until the green beans are crispy and the bacon is cooked through. **7.** Serve hot.

NUTRITIONAL INFORMATION

Per serving: 180 calories, 8g protein, 6g carbohydrates, 14g fat, 3g fiber, 20mg cholesterol, 300mg sodium, 300mg potassium.

Crispy Zucchini Fries

INGREDIENTS:

- 2 medium zucchinis, cut into fry-shaped sticks
- 1/2 cup almond flour
- 1/4 cup grated Parmesan cheese
- 1 tsp garlic powder
- 1/2 tsp paprika
- 1/2 tsp salt
- 1/4 tsp pepper
- 1 large egg, beaten
- Cooking spray or olive oil

Prep Time: 10 min   **Cook Time: 12 min**   **Serves: 4**

DIRECTIONS:

1. Preheat the air fryer to 400°F (200°C). **2.** In one bowl, whisk the egg. In another bowl, mix almond flour, Parmesan cheese, garlic powder, paprika, salt, and pepper. **3.** Dip each zucchini fry into the beaten egg, then coat with the almond flour mixture. **4.** Lightly spray the air fryer basket with cooking spray or olive oil. **5.** Arrange the zucchini fries in a single layer in the air fryer basket. **6.** Cook for 10-12 minutes, flipping halfway through, until golden and crispy. **7.** Remove and serve immediately.

NUTRITIONAL INFORMATION

Per serving: 170 calories, 7g protein, 4g carbohydrates, 13g fat, 2g fiber, 60mg cholesterol, 250mg sodium, 300mg potassium.

Cauliflower Rice with Herbs

INGREDIENTS:

- 1 medium head cauliflower, grated or processed into rice-sized pieces
- 2 tbsp olive oil
- 1 tsp garlic powder
- 1 tsp onion powder
- 1/2 tsp salt
- 1/4 tsp black pepper
- 1 tbsp fresh parsley, chopped
- 1 tbsp fresh cilantro or basil, chopped (optional)
- Lemon wedges for serving (optional)

Prep Time: 10 min   **Cook Time: 10 min**   **Serves: 4**

DIRECTIONS:

1. Preheat the air fryer to 375°F (190°C). **2.** In a large bowl, toss the cauliflower rice with olive oil, garlic powder, onion powder, salt, and pepper. **3.** Lightly spray the air fryer basket with cooking spray or olive oil. **4.** Spread the cauliflower rice evenly in the air fryer basket. **5.** Air fry for 10 minutes, shaking the basket halfway through to ensure even cooking. **6.** Once cooked, transfer the cauliflower rice to a serving dish and stir in the fresh parsley and cilantro (if using). **7.** Serve with a squeeze of lemon for added flavor.

NUTRITIONAL INFORMATION

Per serving: 120 calories, 3g protein, 5g carbohydrates, 10g fat, 3g fiber, 0mg cholesterol, 300mg sodium, 400mg potassium.

Keto Mac and Cheese

INGREDIENTS:

- 1 medium head cauliflower, cut into small florets
- 1 cup shredded cheddar cheese
- 1/2 cup cream cheese, softened
- 1/4 cup heavy cream
- 1/4 cup grated Parmesan cheese
- 1 tsp garlic powder
- 1 tsp onion powder
- Salt and pepper to taste
- 1 tbsp butter
- Cooking spray or olive oil

Prep Time: 10 min   **Cook Time: 12 min**   **Serves: 4**

DIRECTIONS:

1. Preheat the air fryer to 375°F (190°C). **2.** Steam or microwave the cauliflower florets until tender (about 5-7 minutes). Drain any excess water. **3.** In a large bowl, mix the cream cheese, heavy cream, cheddar cheese, Parmesan, garlic powder, onion powder, salt, and pepper. **4.** Add the cooked cauliflower florets to the cheese mixture and stir until well coated. **5.** Transfer the mixture into an oven-safe dish or ramekin. **6.** Place the dish in the air fryer and cook for 10-12 minutes, until the cheese is bubbly and slightly golden. **7.** Let cool for a few minutes before serving.

NUTRITIONAL INFORMATION

Per serving: 310 calories, 10g protein, 6g carbohydrates, 27g fat, 2g fiber, 80mg cholesterol, 450mg sodium, 300mg potassium.

Grilled Asparagus with Lemon Butter

INGREDIENTS:

- 1 lb asparagus, trimmed
- 2 tbsp olive oil
- 2 tbsp butter, melted
- 1 tbsp fresh lemon juice
- 1 tsp lemon zest
- 1 clove garlic, minced
- Salt and pepper to taste
- Cooking spray or olive oil

Prep Time: 5 min   **Cook Time: 10 min**   **Serves: 4**

DIRECTIONS:

1. Preheat the air fryer to 375°F (190°C). **2.** In a bowl, toss the asparagus with olive oil, salt, and pepper. **3.** Lightly spray the air fryer basket with cooking spray or olive oil. **4.** Place the asparagus in a single layer in the air fryer basket. **5.** Air fry for 8-10 minutes, shaking the basket halfway through, until the asparagus is tender and slightly charred. **6.** In a small bowl, mix the melted butter, lemon juice, lemon zest, and garlic. **7.** Drizzle the lemon butter sauce over the cooked asparagus before serving.

NUTRITIONAL INFORMATION

Per serving: 120 calories, 2g protein, 4g carbohydrates, 11g fat, 2g fiber, 15mg cholesterol, 100mg sodium, 250mg potassium.

Broccoli and Cheese Casserole

INGREDIENTS:

- 1 lb broccoli florets
- 1 cup shredded cheddar cheese
- 1/2 cup cream cheese, softened
- 1/4 cup heavy cream
- 1/4 cup grated Parmesan cheese
- 1 tsp garlic powder
- 1 tsp onion powder
- Salt and pepper to taste
- 1 tbsp butter, melted
- Cooking spray or olive oil

Prep Time: 10 min   **cCook Time: 12 min**   **Serves: 4**

DIRECTIONS:

1. Preheat the air fryer to 375°F (190°C). **2.** Steam or microwave the broccoli florets for 5-7 minutes until tender. Drain any excess water. **3.** In a bowl, mix the cream cheese, heavy cream, cheddar cheese, Parmesan, garlic powder, onion powder, salt, and pepper.**4.** Stir the cooked broccoli into the cheese mixture, coating evenly. **5.** Transfer the mixture to an oven-safe dish or ramekin. **6.** Place the dish in the air fryer and cook for 10-12 minutes, until the cheese is bubbly and golden brown. **7.** Let cool for a few minutes before serving.

NUTRITIONAL INFORMATION

Per serving: 320 calories, 12g protein, 7g carbohydrates, 28g fat, 3g fiber, 60mg cholesterol, 400mg sodium, 300mg potassium.

Keto Loaded Baked Avocados

INGREDIENTS:

- 2 ripe avocados, halved and pitted
- 1/2 cup shredded cheddar cheese
- 4 slices cooked bacon, crumbled
- 2 tbsp sour cream
- 1 tbsp fresh chives, chopped
- 1/2 tsp garlic powder
- Salt and pepper to taste
- Cooking spray or olive oil

Prep Time: 5 min   **Cook Time: 8 min**   **Serves: 4**

DIRECTIONS:

1. Preheat the air fryer to 350°F (175°C). **2.** Scoop out a small amount of avocado from the center of each half to create more room for toppings. **3.** Sprinkle the avocado halves with garlic powder, salt, and pepper. **4.** Fill each avocado half with shredded cheese and crumbled bacon. **5.** Lightly spray the air fryer basket with cooking spray or olive oil. **6.** Place the avocados in the air fryer and cook for 6-8 minutes, until the cheese is melted and bubbly. **7.** Remove from the air fryer and top with a dollop of sour cream and fresh chives before serving.

NUTRITIONAL INFORMATION

Per serving: 280 calories, 7g protein, 6g carbohydrates, 24g fat, 8g fiber, 20mg cholesterol, 300mg sodium, 450mg potassium.

Creamed Spinach

INGREDIENTS:

- 10 oz fresh spinach
- 1/2 cup heavy cream
- 1/4 cup cream cheese, softened
- 1/4 cup grated Parmesan cheese
- 1 tbsp butter
- 1/2 tsp garlic powder
- 1/4 tsp nutmeg (optional)
- Salt and pepper to taste
- Cooking spray or olive oil

Prep Time: 5 min   **Cook Time: 10 min**   **Serves: 4**

DIRECTIONS:

1. Preheat the air fryer to 350°F (175°C). **2.** In a pan, melt butter over medium heat. Add fresh spinach and cook for 2-3 minutes until wilted. Drain any excess water. **3.** In a bowl, combine heavy cream, cream cheese, Parmesan cheese, garlic powder, nutmeg (if using), salt, and pepper. Stir in the cooked spinach. **4.** Transfer the mixture to an oven-safe dish or ramekin. **5.** Lightly spray the air fryer basket with cooking spray or olive oil. **6.** Place the dish in the air fryer and cook for 8-10 minutes, until the top is bubbly and slightly golden. **7.** Let cool for a few minutes before serving.

NUTRITIONAL INFORMATION

Per serving: 230 calories, 5g protein, 4g carbohydrates, 21g fat, 2g fiber, 50mg cholesterol, 350mg sodium, 400mg potassium.

Eggplant Parmesan Rounds

INGREDIENTS:

- 1 medium eggplant, sliced into 1/4-inch rounds
- 1/2 cup almond flour
- 1/4 cup grated Parmesan cheese
- 1/2 tsp garlic powder
- 1/2 tsp Italian seasoning
- 1/4 tsp salt
- 1/4 tsp pepper
- 1 large egg, beaten
- 1/2 cup marinara sauce (sugar-free)
- 1/2 cup shredded mozzarella cheese
- Cooking spray or olive oil

Prep Time: 10 min   **Cook Time: 12 min**   **Serves: 4**

DIRECTIONS:

1. Preheat the air fryer to 375°F (190°C). **2.** In a bowl, mix almond flour, Parmesan cheese, garlic powder, Italian seasoning, salt, and pepper. **3.** Dip each eggplant round in the beaten egg, then coat with the almond flour mixture. **4.** Lightly spray the air fryer basket with cooking spray or olive oil. **5.** Place the eggplant rounds in a single layer in the air fryer basket and cook for 8 minutes, flipping halfway through. **6.** Top each eggplant round with a spoonful of marinara sauce and shredded mozzarella. **7.** Return to the air fryer and cook for another 2-4 minutes until the cheese is melted and bubbly.

NUTRITIONAL INFORMATION

Per serving: 250 calories, 10g protein, 7g carbohydrates, 19g fat, 4g fiber, 70mg cholesterol, 400mg sodium, 350mg potassium.

Roasted Bell Peppers with Mozzarella

INGREDIENTS:

- 3 bell peppers (red, yellow, or orange), halved and seeded
- 1 cup shredded mozzarella cheese
- 2 tbsp olive oil
- 1 tsp garlic powder
- 1/2 tsp Italian seasoning
- Salt and pepper to taste
- Fresh basil leaves for garnish (optional)
- Cooking spray or olive oil

Prep Time: 5 min   **Cook Time: 12 min**   **Serves: 4**

DIRECTIONS:

1. Preheat the air fryer to 375°F (190°C). **2.** In a bowl, toss the halved bell peppers with olive oil, garlic powder, Italian seasoning, salt, and pepper. **3.** Lightly spray the air fryer basket with cooking spray or olive oil. **4.** Place the bell peppers cut-side up in the air fryer basket and cook for 8-10 minutes, until tender and slightly charred. **5.** Remove the basket, sprinkle shredded mozzarella cheese inside each pepper half. **6.** Return the peppers to the air fryer and cook for another 2-3 minutes, until the cheese is melted and bubbly. **7.** Garnish with fresh basil leaves before serving (optional).

NUTRITIONAL INFORMATION

Per serving: 180 calories, 6g protein, 7g carbohydrates, 14g fat, 2g fiber, 15mg cholesterol, 200mg sodium, 350mg potassium.

Cheesy Broccoli Tots

INGREDIENTS:

- 1 cup broccoli florets, steamed and finely chopped
- 1/2 cup shredded cheddar cheese
- 1/4 cup almond flour
- 1 large egg, beaten
- 1/4 cup grated Parmesan cheese
- 1/2 tsp garlic powder
- 1/2 tsp onion powder
- Salt and pepper to taste
- Cooking spray or olive oil

Prep Time: 10 min   **Cook Time: 12 min**   **Serves: 4**

DIRECTIONS:

1. Preheat the air fryer to 375°F (190°C). **2.** In a bowl, combine chopped broccoli, cheddar cheese, almond flour, beaten egg, Parmesan cheese, garlic powder, onion powder, salt, and pepper. Mix well to form a dough-like consistency. **3.** Shape the mixture into small tot-shaped pieces. **4.** Lightly spray the air fryer basket with cooking spray or olive oil. **5.** Place the broccoli tots in a single layer in the air fryer basket. **6.** Air fry for 10-12 minutes, shaking the basket halfway through, until golden and crispy on the outside.

NUTRITIONAL INFORMATION

Per serving: 150 calories, 8g protein, 4g carbohydrates, 11g fat, 2g fiber, 50mg cholesterol, 200mg sodium, 250mg potassium.

Baked Avocado with Eggs

INGREDIENTS:

- 2 ripe avocados, halved and pitted
- 4 small eggs
- Salt and pepper to taste
- 1/2 tsp garlic powder
- 1/2 tsp paprika
- 1/4 cup shredded cheddar or mozzarella cheese (optional)
- Fresh parsley or chives for garnish (optional)
- Cooking spray or olive oil

Prep Time: 5 min   **Cook Time: 10 min**   **Serves: 4**

DIRECTIONS:

1. Preheat the air fryer to 350°F (175°C). **2.** Scoop out a small amount of avocado flesh to create more room for the eggs. **3.** Season the avocado halves with garlic powder, paprika, salt, and pepper. **4.** Crack one egg into each avocado half, being careful not to overfill. **5.**Lightly spray the air fryer basket with cooking spray or olive oil. **6.** Place the avocado halves in the air fryer basket and cook for 8-10 minutes, until the eggs are set to your liking. **7.** Optionally, top with shredded cheese in the last 2 minutes of cooking. **8.** Garnish with fresh parsley or chives before serving.

NUTRITIONAL INFORMATION

Per serving: 220 calories, 9g protein, 5g carbohydrates, 18g fat, 7g fiber, 190mg cholesterol, 180mg sodium, 400mg potassium.

Cheesy Broccoli Tots

INGREDIENTS:

- 1 lb Brussels sprouts, halved
- 2 tbsp olive oil
- 3 cloves garlic, minced
- 1/2 tsp garlic powder
- 1/4 tsp paprika (optional)
- Salt and pepper to taste
- 1 tbsp fresh parsley, chopped (optional)
- Cooking spray or olive oil

Prep Time: 5 min   **Cook Time: 15 min**   **Serves: 4**

DIRECTIONS:

1. Preheat the air fryer to 375°F (190°C). **2.** In a large bowl, toss the halved Brussels sprouts with olive oil, minced garlic, garlic powder, paprika, salt, and pepper. **3.** Lightly spray the air fryer basket with cooking spray or olive oil. **4.** Place the Brussels sprouts in a single layer in the air fryer basket. **5.** Air fry for 12-15 minutes, shaking the basket halfway through, until the Brussels sprouts are crispy and golden. **6.** Once done, remove and garnish with fresh parsley if desired.

NUTRITIONAL INFORMATION

Per serving: 130 calories, 4g protein, 8g carbohydrates, 10g fat, 4g fiber, 0mg cholesterol, 180mg sodium, 350mg potassium.

Air-Fried Mushrooms with Feta

INGREDIENTS:

- 1 lb button or cremini mushrooms, cleaned and halved
- 2 tbsp olive oil
- 1 tsp garlic powder
- 1/2 tsp paprika
- Salt and pepper to taste
- 1/2 cup crumbled feta cheese
- 1 tbsp fresh parsley, chopped (optional)
- Cooking spray or olive oil

Prep Time: 5 min   **Cook Time: 12 min**   **Serves: 4**

DIRECTIONS:

1. Preheat the air fryer to 375°F (190°C). **2.** In a bowl, toss the mushrooms with olive oil, garlic powder, paprika, salt, and pepper until evenly coated. **3.** Lightly spray the air fryer basket with cooking spray or olive oil. **4.** Place the mushrooms in a single layer in the air fryer basket. **5.** Air fry for 10-12 minutes, shaking the basket halfway through for even cooking. **6.** Once done, transfer the mushrooms to a serving dish and sprinkle with crumbled feta cheese. **7.** Garnish with fresh parsley if desired.

NUTRITIONAL INFORMATION

Per serving: 140 calories, 5g protein, 5g carbohydrates, 11g fat, 2g fiber, 15mg cholesterol, 280mg sodium, 300mg potassium.

Keto Stuffed Zucchini Boats

INGREDIENTS:

- 2 medium zucchinis, halved lengthwise and scooped out
- 150g ground beef
- 1/4 cup tomato sauce (no sugar added)
- 1/4 cup shredded mozzarella cheese
- 1 tbsp olive oil
- 1/2 tsp garlic powder
- 1/4 tsp salt
- 1/4 tsp black pepper
- Optional: 1 tbsp chopped fresh basil

Prep Time: 10 min   **Cook Time: 12 min**   **Serves: 4**

DIRECTIONS:

1. Preheat the air fryer to 360°F (180°C). **2.** Sauté ground beef with olive oil, garlic powder, salt, and pepper in a pan. **3.** Mix in tomato sauce, then spoon the mixture into the zucchini halves. **4.** Top with shredded cheese and place zucchini boats in the air fryer. **5.** Cook at 360°F (180°C) for 10-12 minutes, until cheese is melted and bubbly. Serving Suggestion: Garnish with fresh basil and serve with a side salad.

NUTRITIONAL INFORMATION

210 calories, 14g protein, 5g carbohydrates, 15g fat, 2g fiber, 30mg cholesterol, 260mg sodium, 350mg potassium.

Garlic Butter Cauliflower Bites

INGREDIENTS:

- 1 medium cauliflower head, cut into florets
- 3 tbsp butter, melted
- 2 cloves garlic, minced
- 1/4 cup grated Parmesan cheese
- 1/2 tsp paprika
- 1/4 tsp salt
- 1/4 tsp black pepper
- Optional: 1 tbsp chopped fresh parsley

Prep Time: 5 min   **Cook Time: 12 min**   **Serves: 4**

DIRECTIONS:

1. Preheat the air fryer to 380°F (190°C). **2.** Toss cauliflower florets with melted butter, garlic, Parmesan, paprika, salt, and pepper. **3.** Place florets in the air fryer basket in a single layer. **4.** Cook at 380°F (190°C) for 10-12 minutes, shaking the basket halfway for even browning. Serving Suggestion: Garnish with parsley and serve with a side of keto-friendly ranch dip.

NUTRITIONAL INFORMATION

160 calories, 4g protein, 5g carbohydrates, 14g fat, 2g fiber, 20mg cholesterol, 180mg sodium, 220mg potassium.

Air-Fried Radishes with Herbs

INGREDIENTS:
- 2 cups radishes, halved
- 2 tbsp olive oil
- 1 tsp dried rosemary
- 1/2 tsp garlic powder
- 1/4 tsp salt
- 1/4 tsp black pepper
- Optional: 1 tbsp chopped fresh parsley

Prep Time: 5 min   **Cook Time: 15 min**   **Serves: 4**

DIRECTIONS:
1. Preheat the air fryer to 400°F (200°C). **2.** Toss radishes with olive oil, rosemary, garlic powder, salt, and pepper. **3.** Arrange radishes in a single layer in the air fryer basket. **4.** Cook at 400°F (200°C) for 12-15 minutes, shaking the basket halfway through.

Serving Suggestion: Garnish with fresh parsley and serve as a side dish with grilled meats.

NUTRITIONAL INFORMATION
80 calories, 1g protein, 4g carbohydrates, 7g fat, 2g fiber, 0mg cholesterol, 180mg sodium, 230mg potassium.

Spinach and Artichoke Stuffed Mushrooms

INGREDIENTS:
- 12 large mushroom caps
- 1/2 cup spinach, chopped
- 1/4 cup canned artichoke hearts, chopped
- 1/4 cup cream cheese, softened
- 1/4 cup shredded mozzarella cheese
- 2 tbsp grated Parmesan cheese
- 1/2 tsp garlic powder
- 1/4 tsp salt
- 1/4 tsp black pepper

Prep Time: 10 min   **Cook Time: 10 min**   **Serves: 4**

DIRECTIONS:
1. Preheat the air fryer to 350°F (180°C). **2.** Mix spinach, artichokes, cream cheese, mozzarella, Parmesan, garlic powder, salt, and pepper. **3.** Spoon the mixture into mushroom caps. **4.** Place stuffed mushrooms in a single layer in the air fryer basket. **5.** Cook at 350°F (180°C) for 8-10 minutes, until cheese is bubbly.

Serving Suggestion: Serve warm, garnished with fresh herbs.

NUTRITIONAL INFORMATION
140 calories, 5g protein, 4g carbohydrates, 11g fat, 1g fiber, 20mg cholesterol, 220mg sodium, 150mg potassium.

Keto Garlic Bread

INGREDIENTS:

- 1 cup almond flour
- 1 1/2 cups shredded mozzarella cheese
- 2 tbsp cream cheese
- 1 large egg
- 1 tsp baking powder
- 1 tsp garlic powder
- 1/2 tsp Italian seasoning
- 2 tbsp butter, melted
- 2 cloves garlic, minced
- 2 tbsp fresh parsley, chopped (optional)
- Cooking spray or olive oil

Prep Time: 10 min   **Cook Time: 10 min**   **Serves: 4**

DIRECTIONS:

1. Preheat the air fryer to 350°F (175°C). **2.** In a microwave-safe bowl, melt the mozzarella and cream cheese together in 30-second intervals until fully melted. **3.** Stir in the almond flour, egg, baking powder, garlic powder, and Italian seasoning to form a dough. **4.** Shape the dough into a loaf or small breadsticks. **5.** Lightly spray the air fryer basket with cooking spray or olive oil. **6.** Place the dough in the air fryer basket and cook for 8-10 minutes, flipping halfway through, until golden and firm. **7.** In a small bowl, mix the melted butter and minced garlic. Brush the garlic butter over the cooked bread. Garnish with fresh parsley, if desired.

NUTRITIONAL INFORMATION

Per serving: 260 calories, 10g protein, 5g carbohydrates, 22g fat, 2g fiber, 80mg cholesterol, 350mg sodium, 150mg potassium.

Air-Fried Almond Flour Bread

INGREDIENTS:

- 1 cup almond flour
- 1 tsp baking powder
- 1/4 tsp salt
- 3 large eggs
- 1/4 cup melted butter or coconut oil
- 1/2 tsp apple cider vinegar
- 1/4 cup shredded cheese (optional for extra flavor)
- Cooking spray or olive oil

Prep Time: 5 min   **Cook Time: 18 min**   **Serves: 4**

DIRECTIONS:

1. Preheat the air fryer to 320°F (160°C). **2.** In a large bowl, whisk together the almond flour, baking powder, and salt. **3.** In a separate bowl, beat the eggs, then stir in the melted butter and apple cider vinegar. **4.** Combine the wet and dry ingredients, mixing until a smooth batter forms. If using shredded cheese, fold it into the batter. **5.** Lightly grease a small loaf pan or ramekin that fits in your air fryer with cooking spray or olive oil. **6.** Pour the batter into the pan and smooth the top. **7.** Air fry for 15-18 minutes, or until the bread is golden and a toothpick inserted comes out clean. **8.** Let the bread cool for a few minutes before slicing and serving.

NUTRITIONAL INFORMATION

Per serving: 250 calories, 9g protein, 5g carbohydrates, 22g fat, 3g fiber, 100mg cholesterol, 300mg sodium, 100mg potassium.

Cheesy Keto Biscuits

INGREDIENTS:

- 1 cup almond flour
- 1/2 cup shredded cheddar cheese
- 2 tbsp cream cheese, softened
- 1 large egg
- 1/2 tsp baking powder
- 1/4 tsp garlic powder (optional)
- 1/4 tsp salt
- 1 tbsp melted butter (for brushing)
- Cooking spray or olive oil

Prep Time: 5 min   **Cook Time: 10 min**   мServes: 6

DIRECTIONS:

1. Preheat the air fryer to 350°F (175°C). **2.** In a medium bowl, mix the almond flour, shredded cheddar cheese, cream cheese, egg, baking powder, garlic powder (if using), and salt until a dough forms. **3.** Divide the dough into 6 equal portions and shape into small biscuit rounds. **4.** Lightly spray the air fryer basket with cooking spray or olive oil. **5.** Place the biscuits in the basket, leaving space between them. **6.** Air fry for 8-10 minutes, flipping halfway through, until golden brown. **7.** Once done, brush the biscuits with melted butter and let cool for a few minutes before serving.

NUTRITIONAL INFORMATION

Per serving: 170 calories, 7g protein, 4g carbohydrates, 14g fat, 2g fiber, 55mg cholesterol, 200mg sodium, 100mg potassium.

Cauliflower Pizza Crust

INGREDIENTS:

- 1 medium head of cauliflower (about 3 cups riced)
- 1/2 cup shredded mozzarella cheese
- 1/4 cup grated Parmesan cheese
- 1 large egg
- 1/2 tsp garlic powder
- 1/2 tsp Italian seasoning
- Salt and pepper to taste
- Cooking spray or olive oil

Prep Time: 10 min   **Cook Time: 12 min**   Serves: 2

DIRECTIONS:

1. Preheat the air fryer to 375°F (190°C). **2.** Process the cauliflower florets in a food processor until it resembles rice. Microwave the cauliflower rice for 4-5 minutes, then let it cool. Use a cheesecloth or a clean kitchen towel to squeeze out as much moisture as possible. **3.** In a bowl, mix the cauliflower, mozzarella, Parmesan, egg, garlic powder, Italian seasoning, salt, and pepper until a dough forms. **4.** Shape the dough into a thin, round pizza crust on parchment paper. **5.** Lightly spray the air fryer basket with cooking spray or olive oil. **6.** Transfer the crust (on parchment paper) into the air fryer basket and cook for 10-12 minutes until the crust is golden and firm. **7.** Once cooked, add your desired keto-friendly toppings and air fry for another 3-4 minutes until the toppings are heated and the cheese is melted.

NUTRITIONAL INFORMATION

Per serv. 170 calories, 10g protein, 6g carbohydrates, 12g fat, 3g fiber, 80mg cholesterol, 250mg sodium, 300mg potassium.

Keto Bagels

INGREDIENTS:

- 1 1/2 cups almond flour
- 2 cups shredded mozzarella cheese
- 2 tbsp cream cheese
- 1 large egg, beaten
- 1 tsp baking powder
- 1/2 tsp garlic powder (optional)
- 1/2 tsp onion powder (optional)
- Sesame seeds or poppy seeds for topping (optional)
- Cooking spray or olive oil

Prep Time: 10 min   Cook Time: 12 min   Serves: 6

DIRECTIONS:

1. Preheat the air fryer to 350°F (175°C). **2.** In a microwave-safe bowl, melt the shredded mozzarella and cream cheese together in 30-second intervals, stirring in between, until fully melted. **3.** In another bowl, mix almond flour, baking powder, garlic powder, and onion powder. Add the melted cheese mixture and the beaten egg. Stir until a dough forms. **4.** Divide the dough into 6 equal parts and shape each into a bagel. **5.** Lightly spray the air fryer basket with cooking spray or olive oil. **6.** Place the bagels in the air fryer, ensuring they don't touch. Air fry for 10-12 minutes, flipping halfway through, until golden brown. **7.** Optionally, sprinkle sesame or poppy seeds on top before air frying.

NUTRITIONAL INFORMATION

Per serving: 290 calories, 12g protein, 5g carbohydrates, 24g fat, 3g fiber, 50mg cholesterol, 270mg sodium, 150mg potassium.

Fathead Pizza with Pepperoni

INGREDIENTS:

- 1 1/2 cups shredded mozzarella cheese
- 2 tbsp cream cheese
- 1 cup almond flour
- 1 large egg, beaten
- 1/2 tsp garlic powder (optional)
- 1/2 tsp Italian seasoning (optional)
- 1/4 cup sugar-free marinara sauce
- 1/2 cup shredded mozzarella cheese (for topping)
- 12 slices pepperoni
- Cooking spray or olive oil

Prep Time: 10 min   Cook Time: 10 min   Serves: 4

DIRECTIONS:

1. Preheat the air fryer to 375°F (190°C). **2.** In a microwave-safe bowl, melt 1 1/2 cups of mozzarella and cream cheese together in 30-second intervals until smooth. **3.** Stir in the almond flour, beaten egg, garlic powder, and Italian seasoning. Mix until dough forms. **4.** Roll the dough between two pieces of parchment paper into a round pizza shape. **5.** Lightly spray the air fryer basket with cooking spray or olive oil, and carefully transfer the dough into the basket. **6.** Air fry for 6-8 minutes until the crust is golden. **7.** Remove the crust, spread marinara sauce, top with 1/2 cup shredded mozzarella, and arrange the pepperoni slices. **8.** Return to the air fryer and cook for another 2-4 minutes until the cheese is melted and bubbly.

NUTRITIONAL INFORMATION

Per serv.: 360 calories, 18g protein, 5g carbohydrates, 30g fat, 2g fiber, 80mg cholesterol, 350mg sodium, 150mg potassium.

Air-Fried Keto Tortillas

INGREDIENTS:

- 1 1/4 cups almond flour
- 1/4 cup coconut flour
- 1 tsp xanthan gum
- 1/4 tsp baking powder
- 1/2 tsp salt
- 1 large egg, beaten
- 2 tbsp olive oil
- 1/4 cup warm water
- Cooking spray or olive oil

Prep Time: 10 min   **Cook Time: 8 min**   **Serves: 4**

DIRECTIONS:

1. In a medium bowl, whisk together the almond flour, coconut flour, xanthan gum, baking powder, and salt. **2.** Stir in the beaten egg and olive oil until well combined. Gradually add warm water until a dough forms. **3.** Divide the dough into 4 equal portions. Roll each portion between two sheets of parchment paper into a thin, round tortilla shape. **4.** Preheat the air fryer to 350°F (175°C). **5.** Lightly spray the air fryer basket with cooking spray or olive oil. **6.** Place one or two tortillas in the air fryer basket, ensuring they don't overlap. Air fry for 3-4 minutes on one side, flip, and cook for an additional 3-4 minutes until golden and crisp. **7.** Repeat for the remaining tortillas.

NUTRITIONAL INFORMATION

Per tortilla: 150 calories, 5g protein, 4g carbohydrates, 12g fat, 3g fiber, 40mg cholesterol, 200mg sodium, 100mg potassium.

Keto Flatbread

INGREDIENTS:

- 1 1/4 cups almond flour
- 1/4 cup coconut flour
- 1 tsp baking powder
- 1/2 tsp salt
- 1/4 cup melted butter or olive oil
- 1 large egg, beaten
- 1/4 cup warm water
- 1/2 tsp garlic powder (optional)
- Cooking spray or olive oil

Prep Time: 10 min   **Cook Time: 8 min**   **Serves: 4**

DIRECTIONS:

1. Preheat the air fryer to 350°F (175°C). **2.** In a medium bowl, mix almond flour, coconut flour, baking powder, salt, and garlic powder (if using). **3.** Add the melted butter and beaten egg to the dry ingredients, stirring to combine. Slowly add the warm water until a dough forms. **4.** Divide the dough into 4 equal portions. Roll each into a thin, flatbread shape between two sheets of parchment paper. **5.** Lightly spray the air fryer basket with cooking spray or olive oil. **6.** Place one or two flatbreads in the air fryer basket, ensuring they don't overlap. Cook for 6-8 minutes, flipping halfway through, until golden and crisp. **7.** Repeat with remaining dough.

NUTRITIONAL INFORMATION

Per serving: 190 calories, 6g protein, 5g carbohydrates, 16g fat, 3g fiber, 50mg cholesterol, 200mg sodium, 100mg potassium.

Low-Carb Mozzarella Pizza

INGREDIENTS:

- 1 1/2 cups shredded mozzarella cheese (for crust)
- 2 tbsp cream cheese
- 3/4 cup almond flour
- 1 large egg, beaten
- 1/2 tsp garlic powder (optional)
- 1/2 tsp Italian seasoning (optional)
- 1/4 cup sugar-free marinara sauce
- 1/2 cup shredded mozzarella cheese (for topping)
- Optional toppings: pepperoni, olives, bell peppers, mushrooms
- Cooking spray or olive oil

Prep Time: 10 min   **Cook Time: 12 min**   **Serves: 2**

DIRECTIONS:

1. Preheat the air fryer to 375°F (190°C). **2.** In a microwave-safe bowl, melt 1 1/2 cups mozzarella cheese and cream cheese in 30-second intervals, stirring in between until smooth. **3.** Stir in the almond flour, beaten egg, garlic powder, and Italian seasoning until a dough forms. **4.** Roll the dough between two sheets of parchment paper into a pizza crust shape. **5.** Lightly spray the air fryer basket with cooking spray or olive oil. **6.** Transfer the crust (with parchment paper) to the air fryer basket and cook for 6-8 minutes until golden. **7.** Remove the crust, spread marinara sauce, top with shredded mozzarella and any optional toppings. **8.** Return to the air fryer and cook for another 3-4 minutes until the cheese is melted and bubbly.

NUTRITIONAL INFORMATION

Per serving: 350 calories, 20g protein, 6g carbohydrates, 28g fat, 2g fiber, 120mg cholesterol, 450mg sodium, 100mg potassium.

Coconut Flour Bread Rolls

INGREDIENTS:

- 1/2 cup coconut flour
- 4 large eggs
- 1/4 cup melted butter or coconut oil
- 1 tsp baking powder
- 1/2 tsp salt
- 1/2 tsp garlic powder (optional)
- 1/4 cup shredded cheese (optional for extra flavor)
- 1 tbsp psyllium husk powder (optional for texture)
- Cooking spray or olive oil

Prep Time: 10 min   **Cook Time:12 min**   **Serves: 6**

DIRECTIONS:

1. Preheat the air fryer to 350°F (175°C). **2.** In a bowl, whisk the eggs until smooth. Stir in the melted butter (or coconut oil), coconut flour, baking powder, salt, garlic powder (if using), and psyllium husk powder. **3.** Mix until a dough forms. If adding shredded cheese, fold it in now. **4.** Divide the dough into 6 equal portions and roll them into round shapes. **5.** Lightly spray the air fryer basket with cooking spray or olive oil. **6.** Place the rolls in the air fryer, ensuring they don't touch. Cook for 10-12 minutes, flipping halfway through, until golden brown and firm to the touch. **7.** Let cool for a few minutes before serving.

NUTRITIONAL INFORMATION

Per serving: 120 calories, 6g protein, 4g carbohydrates, 9g fat, 3g fiber, 110mg cholesterol, 220mg sodium, 100mg potassium.

Air-Fried Pizza Pockets

INGREDIENTS:

- 1 1/2 cups shredded mozzarella cheese (for dough)
- 2 tbsp cream cheese
- 1 cup almond flour
- 1 large egg, beaten
- 1/2 tsp garlic powder (optional)
- 1/2 tsp Italian seasoning
- 1/4 cup sugar-free marinara sauce
- 1/2 cup shredded mozzarella cheese (for filling)
- 12 slices pepperoni (optional)
- Cooking spray or olive oil

Prep Time: 10 min **Cook Time: 10 min** **Serves: 4**

DIRECTIONS:

1. Preheat the air fryer to 375°F (190°C). **2.** In a microwave-safe bowl, melt 1 1/2 cups of mozzarella and cream cheese in 30-second intervals, stirring in between, until smooth. **3.** Stir in the almond flour, beaten egg, garlic powder, and Italian seasoning until dough forms. **4.** Divide the dough into 4 equal portions and roll each out into a small rectangle between two sheets of parchment paper. **5.** On one side of each rectangle, spread a small amount of marinara sauce, top with shredded mozzarella, and add pepperoni if desired. Fold the dough over to create a pocket and press the edges to seal. **6.** Lightly spray the air fryer basket with cooking spray. Place the pizza pockets in the basket and air fry for 8-10 minutes, flipping halfway through, until golden and crispy.

NUTRITIONAL INFORMATION

Per serving: 320 calories, 20g protein, 7g carbohydrates, 25g fat, 3g fiber, 80mg cholesterol, 450mg sodium, 150mg potassium.

Air-Fried Keto Garlic Knots

INGREDIENTS:

- 1 1/2 cups shredded mozzarella cheese
- 2 tbsp cream cheese
- 1 cup almond flour
- 1 large egg, beaten
- 1/2 tsp garlic powder
- 1/2 tsp Italian seasoning
- 2 tbsp melted butter
- 2 cloves garlic, minced
- 1 tbsp chopped fresh parsley (optional)
- Cooking spray or olive oil

Prep Time: 10 min **Cook Time:10 min** **Serves: 6**

DIRECTIONS:

1. Preheat the air fryer to 375°F (190°C). **2.** In a microwave-safe bowl, melt the shredded mozzarella and cream cheese in 30-second intervals until smooth. **3.** Stir in almond flour, beaten egg, garlic powder, and Italian seasoning until a dough forms. **4.** Divide the dough into 6 equal portions. Roll each portion into a long strip and gently tie into a knot. **5.** Lightly spray the air fryer basket with cooking spray. Place the garlic knots in the basket, ensuring they don't overlap. **6.** Air fry for 8-10 minutes, flipping halfway through, until golden brown. **7.** While the knots are cooking, mix the melted butter, minced garlic, and parsley. **8.** Once the garlic knots are done, brush them with the garlic butter mixture.

NUTRITIONAL INFORMATION

Per serving: 180 calories, 10g protein, 5g carbohydrates, 15g fat, 2g fiber, 45mg cholesterol, 200mg sodium, 120mg potassium.

INGREDIENTS:

- 1 cup almond flour
- 1/4 cup coconut flour
- 1/4 cup granulated erythritol
- 1 tsp baking powder
- 1/2 tsp cinnamon
- 3 large eggs
- 1/4 cup unsweetened almond milk
- 2 tbsp melted butter
- 1/2 tsp vanilla extract
- For coating: 2 tbsp melted butter, 1/4 cup erythritol, 1 tsp cinnamon

Prep Time: 10 min   **Cook Time: 8 min**   **Serves: 6 donuts**

DIRECTIONS:

1. Preheat the air fryer to 350°F (180°C). **2.** Mix almond flour, coconut flour, erythritol, baking powder, and cinnamon. **3.** Add eggs, almond milk, melted butter, and vanilla; mix until smooth. **4.** Fill silicone donut molds with batter. **5.** Air fry at 350°F (180°C) for 6-8 minutes, until golden. **6.** Brush warm donuts with melted butter and roll in the cinnamon-erythritol mixture.

Serving Suggestion: Enjoy warm with a keto-friendly coffee.

NUTRITIONAL INFORMATION

180 calories, 6g protein, 4g carbohydrates, 15g fat, 3g fiber, 60mg cholesterol, 80mg sodium, 50mg potassium.

Low-Carb Herb Focaccia

INGREDIENTS:

- 1 cup almond flour
- 1/4 cup coconut flour
- 1/4 cup grated Parmesan cheese
- 1 tsp baking powder
- 1 tsp dried rosemary
- 1 tsp dried thyme
- 2 large eggs
- 1/4 cup olive oil
- 1/4 cup warm water
- 1/2 tsp garlic powder
- 1/4 tsp salt
- Optional: sea salt flakes for topping

Prep Time: 10 min   **Cook Time:12 min**   **Serves: 6**

DIRECTIONS:

1. Preheat the air fryer to 350°F (180°C). **2.** Mix almond flour, coconut flour, Parmesan, baking powder, rosemary, thyme, garlic powder, and salt. **3.** Add eggs, olive oil, and water; mix into a dough. **4.** Press dough into a flat round shape and place in the air fryer. **5.** Cook at 350°F (180°C) for 10-12 minutes, shaking halfway.

Serving Suggestion: Serve with a side of olive oil and balsamic vinegar for dipping.

NUTRITIONAL INFORMATION

210 calories, 6g protein, 4g carbohydrates, 19g fat, 3g fiber, 40mg cholesterol, 150mg sodium, 80mg potassium.

Cheesy Keto Breadsticks

INGREDIENTS:

- 1 cup shredded mozzarella cheese
- 1/2 cup almond flour
- 1/4 cup grated Parmesan cheese
- 1 large egg
- 1/2 tsp garlic powder
- 1/2 tsp dried oregano
- 1/4 tsp salt
- Optional: 1 tbsp chopped fresh basil for garnish

Prep Time: 5 min   **Cook Time: 10 min**   **Serves: 6**

DIRECTIONS:

1. Preheat the air fryer to 350°F (180°C). **2.** Mix mozzarella, almond flour, Parmesan, egg, garlic powder, oregano, and salt into a dough. **3.** Form dough into a rectangular shape on parchment paper. **4.** Place in the air fryer and cook at 350°F (180°C) for 8-10 minutes, until golden. **5.** Tip: Flip the breadsticks halfway through cooking for even browning. Serving Suggestion: Serve with a side of marinara sauce or pesto.

NUTRITIONAL INFORMATION

180 calories, 10g protein, 3g carbohydrates, 14g fat, 1g fiber, 45mg cholesterol, 220mg sodium, 60mg potassium.

Stuffed Keto Pretzel Bites

INGREDIENTS:

- 1 cup almond flour
- 1 1/2 cups shredded mozzarella cheese
- 2 tbsp cream cheese
- 1 large egg
- 1/2 tsp baking powder
- 1/4 tsp salt
- 1/4 cup stuffed filling (cheddar cubes or sausage bits)
- Optional: coarse salt for topping

Prep Time: 10 min   **Cook Time:8 min**   **Serves: 6**

DIRECTIONS:

1. Preheat the air fryer to 370°F (190°C). **2.** Melt mozzarella and cream cheese; mix in almond flour, egg, baking powder, and salt to form dough. **3.** Divide dough into small balls, stuff each with cheddar or sausage. **4.** Place bites in the air fryer and cook at 370°F (190°C) for 6-8 minutes, shaking halfway.

Serving Suggestion: Serve with keto-friendly mustard or cheese dip.

NUTRITIONAL INFORMATION

190 calories, 9g protein, 4g carbohydrates, 15g fat, 2g fiber, 35mg cholesterol, 280mg sodium, 60mg potassium.

Air-Fried Keto Calzones

INGREDIENTS:

- 1 1/2 cups shredded mozzarella cheese
- 2 tbsp cream cheese
- 1 cup almond flour
- 1 large egg
- 1/4 cup marinara sauce (sugar-free)
- 1/2 cup cooked sausage or pepperoni slices
- 1/4 cup shredded mozzarella (for filling)
- 1/2 tsp Italian seasoning
- Optional: 1 tbsp grated Parmesan for topping

Prep Time: 10 min   **Cook Time: 10 min**   **Serves: 4**

DIRECTIONS:

1. Preheat the air fryer to 375°F (190°C). **2.** Melt mozzarella and cream cheese; combine with almond flour and egg to form dough. **3.** Roll dough into circles, fill with marinara, sausage/pepperoni, and cheese. **4.** Fold into calzones, sealing edges. Cook at 375°F (190°C) for 8-10 minutes.

Serving Suggestion: Serve with a side of marinara sauce for dipping.

NUTRITIONAL INFORMATION

300 calories, 16g protein, 5g carbohydrates, 24g fat, 2g fiber, 55mg cholesterol, 410mg sodium, 150mg potassium.

Garlic and Rosemary Keto Flatbread

INGREDIENTS:

- 1 cup almond flour
- 1/4 cup coconut flour
- 1/2 cup shredded mozzarella cheese
- 2 tbsp cream cheese
- 1 large egg
- 1 tbsp olive oil
- 1 tsp dried rosemary
- 1/2 tsp garlic powder
- 1/4 tsp salt
- Optional: sea salt flakes for topping

Prep Time: 10 min   **Cook Time:10 min**   **Serves: 4**

DIRECTIONS:

1. Preheat the air fryer to 350°F (180°C). **2.** Melt mozzarella and cream cheese; mix with almond flour, coconut flour, egg, olive oil, rosemary, garlic powder, and salt to form dough. **3.** Press dough into a flat circle on parchment paper. **4.** Cook in the air fryer at 350°F (180°C) for 8-10 minutes, flipping halfway.

Serving Suggestion: Serve warm with a side of olive oil for dipping.

NUTRITIONAL INFORMATION

210 calories, 7g protein, 5g carbohydrates, 18g fat, 3g fiber, 40mg cholesterol, 170mg sodium, 80mg potassium.

Keto Cheese and Herb Biscuits

INGREDIENTS:

- 1 cup almond flour
- 1/2 cup shredded cheddar cheese
- 2 tbsp cream cheese, softened
- 1 large egg
- 1/2 tsp baking powder
- 1/2 tsp dried rosemary
- 1/2 tsp dried thyme
- 1/4 tsp garlic powder
- 1/4 tsp salt

Prep Time: 5 min   **Cook Time: 10 min**   **Serves: 6**

DIRECTIONS:

1. Preheat the air fryer to 350°F (180°C). **2.** Mix almond flour, cheddar, cream cheese, egg, baking powder, rosemary, thyme, garlic powder, and salt into a dough. **3.** Form small biscuit shapes and place them in a single layer in the air fryer. **4.** Cook at 350°F (180°C) for 8-10 minutes, flipping halfway for even browning.

Serving Suggestion: Serve warm with a side of butter or low-carb gravy.

NUTRITIONAL INFORMATION

150 calories, 7g protein, 4g carbohydrates, 12g fat, 2g fiber, 30mg cholesterol, 180mg sodium, 50mg potassium.

Low-Carb Cauliflower Breadsticks

INGREDIENTS:

- 2 cups riced cauliflower
- 1/2 cup shredded mozzarella cheese
- 1/4 cup grated Parmesan cheese
- 1 large egg
- 1/2 tsp garlic powder
- 1/2 tsp dried oregano
- 1/4 tsp salt
- Optional: 1 tbsp chopped fresh basil for garnish

Prep Time: 10 min   **Cook Time:12 min**   **Serves: 4**

DIRECTIONS:

1. Preheat the air fryer to 375°F (190°C). **2.** Microwave cauliflower for 5 minutes; drain excess moisture. **3.** Mix cauliflower, mozzarella, Parmesan, egg, garlic powder, oregano, and salt. **4.** Form dough into a rectangle and place it in the air fryer. **5.** Cook at 375°F (190°C) for 10-12 minutes, flipping halfway.

Serving Suggestion: Serve with marinara sauce or olive oil for dipping.

NUTRITIONAL INFORMATION

120 calories, 8g protein, 5g carbohydrates, 7g fat, 2g fiber, 40mg cholesterol, 200mg sodium, 150mg potassium.

Chapter 8: Desserts and Sweet Treats

Keto Chocolate Chip Cookies

INGREDIENTS:

- 1 1/2 cups almond flour
- 1/4 cup coconut flour
- 1/2 cup unsalted butter, softened
- 1/2 cup erythritol or keto-friendly sweetener
- 1 large egg
- 1 tsp vanilla extract
- 1/2 tsp baking powder
- 1/4 tsp salt
- 1/2 cup sugar-free chocolate chips
- Cooking spray or olive oil

Prep Time: 10 min   **Cook Time: 8 min**   **Serves: 12 cookies**

DIRECTIONS:

1. Preheat the air fryer to 350°F (175°C). **2.** In a bowl, cream together the softened butter and erythritol until smooth. Beat in the egg and vanilla extract. **3.** In a separate bowl, whisk together the almond flour, coconut flour, baking powder, and salt. Gradually add the dry ingredients to the wet ingredients, mixing until a dough forms. **4.** Fold in the sugar-free chocolate chips. **5.** Lightly spray the air fryer basket with cooking spray or olive oil. **6.** Roll the dough into 12 small balls, flatten slightly, and place in the air fryer basket, ensuring they are spaced out. **7.** Air fry for 6-8 minutes, until golden brown on the edges. Flip halfway through for even cooking. **8.** Let the cookies cool for a few minutes before serving, as they will firm up while cooling.

NUTRITIONAL INFORMATION

Per serving: 140 calories, 4g protein, 5g carbohydrates, 12g fat, 2g fiber, 25mg cholesterol, 90mg sodium, 60mg potassium.

Almond Flour Brownies

INGREDIENTS:

- 3/4 cup almond flour
- 1/4 cup unsweetened cocoa powder
- 1/4 cup erythritol or keto-friendly sweetener
- 2 tbsp melted butter or coconut oil
- 1 large egg
- 1/2 tsp vanilla extract
- 1/4 tsp baking powder
- Pinch of salt
- 2 tbsp sugar-free chocolate chips (optional)
- Cooking spray or olive oil

Prep Time: 10 min   **Cook Time:14 min**   **Serves: 4**

DIRECTIONS:

1. Preheat the air fryer to 320°F (160°C). **2.** In a bowl, whisk together the almond flour, cocoa powder, erythritol, baking powder, and salt. **3.** In a separate bowl, beat the egg, then add the melted butter (or coconut oil) and vanilla extract. Mix well. **4.** Gradually stir the dry ingredients into the wet mixture until smooth. Fold in the sugar-free chocolate chips, if desired. **5.** Lightly grease a small air fryer-safe baking dish or line with parchment paper. Pour the batter into the dish and smooth the top. **6.** Place the dish in the air fryer and cook for 12-14 minutes, or until a toothpick inserted into the center comes out mostly clean. **7.** Allow the brownies to cool slightly before cutting.

NUTRITIONAL INFORMATION

170 calories, 6g protein, 5g carbohydrates, 15g fat, 3g fiber, 35mg cholesterol, 120mg sodium, 100mg potassium.

Air-Fried Cinnamon Donuts

INGREDIENTS:

- 1 1/2 cups almond flour
- 1/4 cup coconut flour
- 1/4 cup erythritol or keto-friendly sweetener
- 1/2 tsp baking powder
- 1/4 tsp salt
- 1/2 tsp cinnamon
- 2 large eggs
- 1/4 cup unsweetened almond milk
- 1/4 cup melted butter
- 1/2 tsp vanilla extract
- 1 tbsp erythritol mixed with 1/2 tsp cinnamon for coating

Prep Time: 10 min   **Cook Time: 10 min**   **Serves: 6 donuts**

DIRECTIONS:

1. Preheat the air fryer to 350°F (175°C). **2.** In a bowl, mix almond flour, coconut flour, erythritol, baking powder, salt, and cinnamon. **3.** In another bowl, whisk together eggs, almond milk, melted butter, and vanilla extract. **4.** Gradually combine the dry ingredients with the wet ingredients, mixing until a dough forms. **5.** Shape the dough into 6 small donuts. **6.**Lightly grease the air fryer basket with cooking spray. Place the donuts in the basket, making sure they don't overlap. **7.** Air fry for 8-10 minutes, flipping halfway through, until golden brown. **8.** Remove the donuts from the air fryer and let cool for a couple of minutes. **9.** Toss the donuts in the cinnamon-erythritol mixture to coat.

NUTRITIONAL INFORMATION

200 calories, 7g protein, 4g carbohydrates, 18g fat, 3g fiber, 50mg cholesterol, 150mg sodium, 100mg potassium.

Keto Cheesecake Bites

INGREDIENTS:

- 1 1/2 cups cream cheese, softened
- 1/4 cup erythritol or keto-friendly sweetener
- 1 large egg
- 1 tsp vanilla extract
- 1/2 cup almond flour
- 2 tbsp butter, melted
- 1/4 tsp cinnamon (optional)
- Cooking spray or olive oil

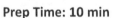

Prep Time: 10 min   **Cook Time:10 min**   **6 cheesecake bites**

DIRECTIONS:

1. Preheat the air fryer to 320°F (160°C). **2.** In a bowl, mix the cream cheese, erythritol, egg, and vanilla extract until smooth. **3.** In a separate bowl, combine the almond flour, melted butter, and cinnamon (if using) to form the crust mixture. **4.** Lightly grease silicone molds or small ramekins with cooking spray. **5.** Press a small amount of the almond flour crust mixture into the bottom of each mold. **6.** Spoon the cheesecake filling on top of the crust, filling each mold about 3/4 full. **7.** Place the molds in the air fryer and cook for 8-10 minutes until the edges are set but the center is slightly jiggly. **8.** Let the cheesecake bites cool before removing them from the molds. Refrigerate for at least 1 hour before serving.

NUTRITIONAL INFORMATION

210 calories, 5g protein, 4g carbohydrates, 20g fat, 2g fiber, 60mg cholesterol, 140mg sodium, 90mg potassium.

Lemon Blueberry Mug Cake

INGREDIENTS:

- 3 tbsp almond flour
- 1 tbsp coconut flour
- 1 tbsp erythritol or keto-friendly sweetener
- 1/4 tsp baking powder
- 1 large egg
- 2 tbsp unsweetened almond milk
- 1 tbsp melted butter
- 1/2 tsp vanilla extract
- 1/2 tsp lemon zest
- 1 tbsp fresh or frozen blueberries
- Cooking spray or olive oil

Prep Time: 5 min   **Cook Time: 8 min**   **Serves: 1 mug cake**

DIRECTIONS:

1. Preheat the air fryer to 350°F (175°C). **2.** In a small bowl, mix almond flour, coconut flour, erythritol, and baking powder. **3.** In another bowl, whisk the egg, almond milk, melted butter, vanilla extract, and lemon zest. **4.** Combine the dry ingredients with the wet mixture until smooth. **5.** Gently fold in the blueberries. **6.** Lightly grease an air fryer-safe mug or small ramekin with cooking spray. Pour the batter into the mug, filling it about 3/4 of the way. **7.** Place the mug in the air fryer and cook for 6-8 minutes, checking for doneness by inserting a toothpick in the center. **8.** Let cool slightly before serving.

NUTRITIONAL INFORMATION

210 calories, 8g protein, 6g carbohydrates, 18g fat, 3g fiber, 65mg cholesterol, 120mg sodium, 110mg potassium.

Chocolate Lava Cake

INGREDIENTS:

- 1/4 cup almond flour
- 2 tbsp unsweetened cocoa powder
- 2 tbsp erythritol or keto-friendly sweetener
- 1 large egg
- 2 tbsp melted butter
- 1/4 tsp baking powder
- 1/2 tsp vanilla extract
- 1 oz sugar-free dark chocolate
- Cooking spray or olive oil

Prep Time: 5 min   **Cook Time:8 min**   **Serves: 2**

DIRECTIONS:

1. Preheat the air fryer to 350°F (175°C). **2.** In a small bowl, mix almond flour, cocoa powder, erythritol, and baking powder. **3.** In a separate bowl, whisk the egg, melted butter, and vanilla extract. **4.** Combine the dry ingredients with the wet mixture until smooth. **5.** Grease two small ramekins with cooking spray. Divide the batter between the ramekins. **6.** Press a small piece of sugar-free dark chocolate into the center of each ramekin, ensuring it's fully covered by the batter. **7.** Air fry the cakes for 6-8 minutes until the edges are set but the center remains slightly soft. **8.** Let cool for 1-2 minutes before serving.

NUTRITIONAL INFORMATION

250 calories, 7g protein, 5g carbohydrates, 23g fat, 3g fiber, 70mg cholesterol, 120mg sodium, 90mg potassium.

Coconut Macaroons

INGREDIENTS:
- 2 cups unsweetened shredded coconut
- 1/3 cup erythritol or keto-friendly sweetener
- 2 large egg whites
- 1/4 cup almond flour
- 1/2 tsp vanilla extract
- Pinch of salt
- Cooking spray or olive oil

Prep Time: 10 min **Cook Time: 10 min** **12 macaroons**

DIRECTIONS:
1. Preheat the air fryer to 320°F (160°C). **2.** In a large bowl, whisk the egg whites until frothy. **3.** Add erythritol, almond flour, vanilla extract, and salt to the egg whites. Mix until fully combined. **4.** Gently fold in the shredded coconut until the mixture forms a sticky dough. **5.** Form small balls or mounds (about 1 tablespoon each) with the coconut mixture. **6.** Lightly grease the air fryer basket with cooking spray and place the macaroons in a single layer, leaving some space between them. **7.** Air fry for 8-10 minutes, until golden and slightly crispy on the outside. **8.** Let the macaroons cool for a few minutes before removing them from the air fryer.

NUTRITIONAL INFORMATION
110 calories, 2g protein, 3g carbohydrates, 10g fat, 2g fiber, 0mg cholesterol, 50mg sodium, 60mg potassium.

Air-Fried Keto Apple Fritters

INGREDIENTS:
- 1 cup almond flour
- 2 tbsp coconut flour
- 2 tbsp erythritol or keto-friendly sweetener
- 1 tsp cinnamon
- 1 tsp baking powder
- 2 large eggs
- 1/4 cup unsweetened almond milk
- 1/2 tsp vanilla extract
- 1 small zucchini, peeled and diced (as apple substitute)
- 1 tbsp melted butter
- Cooking spray or olive oil

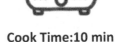

Prep Time: 10 min **Cook Time:10 min** **Serves: 6**

DIRECTIONS:
1. Preheat the air fryer to 350°F (175°C). **2.** In a large bowl, combine almond flour, coconut flour, erythritol, cinnamon, and baking powder. **3.** In another bowl, whisk the eggs, almond milk, melted butter, and vanilla extract. **4.** Mix the wet ingredients into the dry ingredients until a thick batter forms. **5.** Fold in the diced zucchini to mimic apple texture. **6.** Grease the air fryer basket with cooking spray. Spoon the batter into small rounds, leaving space between fritters. **7.** Air fry for 8-10 minutes, flipping halfway through, until golden brown and crispy. **8.** Let cool slightly before serving.

NUTRITIONAL INFORMATION
140 calories, 5g protein, 4g carbohydrates, 11g fat, 2g fiber, 45mg cholesterol, 95mg sodium, 120mg potassium.

Peanut Butter Cookies

INGREDIENTS:

- 1 cup natural peanut butter (unsweetened, no added sugar)
- 1/3 cup erythritol or keto-friendly sweetener
- 1 large egg
- 1/2 tsp vanilla extract
- 1/4 tsp baking powder
- Pinch of salt
- Cooking spray or olive oil

Prep Time: 5 min **Cook Time: 8 min** **Serves: 12 cookies**

DIRECTIONS:

1. Preheat the air fryer to 350°F (175°C). **2.** In a medium bowl, mix together the peanut butter, erythritol, egg, vanilla extract, baking powder, and a pinch of salt until a smooth dough forms. **3.** Form small balls of dough (about 1 tablespoon each) and slightly flatten with a fork, creating a crisscross pattern on top. **4.** Grease the air fryer basket with cooking spray and place the cookies in a single layer, leaving space between them. **5.** Air fry for 6-8 minutes, or until the edges are golden and firm. **6.** Allow the cookies to cool for a few minutes before removing them from the air fryer.

NUTRITIONAL INFORMATION

140 calories, 5g protein, 3g carbohydrates, 12g fat, 2g fiber, 25mg cholesterol, 100mg sodium, 90mg potassium.

Almond Joy Fat Bombs

INGREDIENTS:

- 1/2 cup coconut oil
- 1/2 cup unsweetened shredded coconut
- 1/4 cup almond butter
- 2 tbsp erythritol or keto-friendly sweetener
- 1/4 cup unsweetened cocoa powder
- 1/2 tsp vanilla extract
- 12 whole almonds
- Cooking spray or olive oil

Prep Time: 10 min **Cook Time:5 min** **Serves: 12 fat bombs**

DIRECTIONS:

1. In a bowl, mix the coconut oil, almond butter, shredded coconut, erythritol, cocoa powder, and vanilla extract until well combined. **2.** Shape the mixture into small balls and gently press an almond into the center of each ball. **3.** Place the fat bombs in the freezer for 10 minutes to firm up. **4.** Preheat the air fryer to 300°F (150°C). Lightly grease the basket with cooking spray. **5.** Air fry the fat bombs for 4-5 minutes, checking halfway through. Be cautious not to overheat the fat bombs; they should just firm up. **6.** Allow them to cool before serving.

NUTRITIONAL INFORMATION

140 calories, 2g protein, 3g carbohydrates, 13g fat, 2g fiber, 0mg cholesterol, 15mg sodium, 45mg potassium.

Chocolate Coconut Bars

INGREDIENTS:
- 1 cup unsweetened shredded coconut
- 1/2 cup coconut oil
- 1/4 cup almond flour
- 2 tbsp erythritol or keto-friendly sweetener
- 1/2 cup sugar-free dark chocolate chips
- 1/2 tsp vanilla extract
- Pinch of salt
- Cooking spray

Prep Time: 10 min **Cook Time: 5 min** **Serves: 8 bars**

DIRECTIONS:
1. In a bowl, mix the shredded coconut, almond flour, erythritol, coconut oil, vanilla extract, and a pinch of salt until fully combined. **2.** Press the mixture evenly into a small, greased air fryer-safe baking dish. **3.** Preheat the air fryer to 300°F (150°C).**4.** Air fry the mixture for 5 minutes or until the edges are golden. **5.** Melt the sugar-free dark chocolate chips in the microwave and spread evenly over the coconut base. **6.** Let the bars cool in the fridge for 30 minutes before cutting into squares.

NUTRITIONAL INFORMATION
180 calories, 3g protein, 5g carbohydrates, 17g fat, 3g fiber, 0mg cholesterol, 10mg sodium, 60mg potassium.

Keto Pumpkin Pie

INGREDIENTS:
- **For the Crust:**
- 1 cup almond flour
- 2 tbsp coconut flour
- 1/4 cup melted butter
- 1 tbsp erythritol or keto-friendly sweetener
- 1/4 tsp salt
- **For the Filling:**
- 1 cup pumpkin puree (unsweetened)
- 1/2 cup heavy cream
- 1/4 cup erythritol or keto-friendly sweetener
- 2 large eggs
- 1 tsp vanilla extract
- 1 tsp ground cinnamon
- 1/2 tsp ground ginger
- 1/4 tsp ground nutmeg
- Pinch of salt

Prep Time: 15 min **Cook Time:25 min** **Serves: 6**

DIRECTIONS:
1. In a bowl, mix almond flour, coconut flour, melted butter, erythritol, and salt until it forms a crumbly dough. **2.** Press the dough into a greased air fryer-safe pie dish. Set aside. **3.** In another bowl, whisk together pumpkin puree, heavy cream, erythritol, eggs, vanilla extract, and spices until smooth. **4.** Pour the filling into the prepared crust. **5.** Preheat air fryer to 320°F (160°C). Air fry the pie for 20-25 minutes, or until the center is set. If the crust browns too quickly, cover with foil halfway through cooking. **6.** Let cool for 10 minutes before slicing.

NUTRITIONAL INFORMATION
210 calories, 5g protein, 7g carbohydrates, 18g fat, 3g fiber, 70mg cholesterol, 120mg sodium, 150mg potassium.

Coconut Flour Chocolate Cake

INGREDIENTS:

- 1/2 cup coconut flour
- 1/4 cup unsweetened cocoa powder
- 1/2 cup erythritol or keto-friendly sweetener
- 1/2 tsp baking powder
- 1/4 tsp salt
- 4 large eggs
- 1/3 cup melted coconut oil or butter
- 1/2 cup unsweetened almond milk
- 1 tsp vanilla extract

Prep Time: 10 min   **Cook Time: 20 min**   **Serves: 6**

DIRECTIONS:

1. In a bowl, whisk coconut flour, cocoa powder, erythritol, baking powder, and salt. **2.** In a separate bowl, beat eggs, melted coconut oil (or butter), almond milk, and vanilla extract. **3.** Gradually add the dry ingredients to the wet mixture, stirring until smooth. **4.** Pour the batter into a greased, air fryer-safe cake pan. **5.** Preheat the air fryer to 320°F (160°C). Air fry for 18-20 minutes. Check for doneness by inserting a toothpick into the center; it should come out clean. **6.** Let cool for 10 minutes before slicing.

NUTRITIONAL INFORMATION

180 calories, 6g protein, 5g carbohydrates, 14g fat, 3g fiber, 95mg cholesterol, 120mg sodium, 170mg potassium.

Creamy Keto Tiramisu

INGREDIENTS:

- **For the cake layer:**
- 1/2 cup almond flour
- 2 tbsp coconut flour
- 1/4 cup erythritol
- 1/2 tsp baking powder
- 3 large eggs
- 2 tbsp melted butter
- 1/4 cup unsweetened almond milk
- 1 tsp vanilla extract
- **For the filling:**
- 1 cup mascarpone cheese
- 1/2 cup heavy cream
- 2 tbsp powdered erythritol
- 1 tsp vanilla extract
- 1/2 cup brewed coffee
- Unsweetened cocoa powder (for dusting)

Prep Time: 15 min   **Cook Time:10 min**   **Serves: 4**

DIRECTIONS:

1. In a bowl, mix almond flour, coconut flour, erythritol, and baking powder. In another bowl, whisk eggs, melted butter, almond milk, and vanilla. Combine wet and dry ingredients. **2.** Pour the batter into a greased air fryer-safe pan. Preheat air fryer to 320°F (160°C). Cook for 8-10 minutes until the cake is firm. Cool, then slice into layers. **3.** Whip the mascarpone, heavy cream, powdered erythritol, and vanilla until smooth. **4.** Dip cake layers in brewed coffee and layer with the cream mixture. **5.** Dust with cocoa powder before serving.

NUTRITIONAL INFORMATION

290 calories, 7g protein, 5g carbohydrates, 26g fat, 2g fiber, 135mg cholesterol, 90mg sodium, 110mg potassium.

Air-Fried Churros

INGREDIENTS:

- 1/2 cup almond flour
- 1/4 cup coconut flour
- 2 tbsp powdered erythritol (plus extra for dusting)
- 1/2 tsp baking powder
- 1/2 tsp cinnamon (plus extra for dusting)
- 1/4 tsp xanthan gum
- 2 large eggs
- 1/4 cup butter, melted
- 1 tsp vanilla extract
- 2 tbsp water

Prep Time: 10 min   **Cook Time: 12 min**   **Serves: 4**

DIRECTIONS:

1. In a bowl, mix almond flour, coconut flour, erythritol, baking powder, cinnamon, and xanthan gum. **2.** In a separate bowl, whisk together eggs, melted butter, vanilla extract, and water. Add the wet mixture to the dry ingredients and combine to form a dough. **3.** Preheat your air fryer to 350°F (175°C). **4.** Transfer the dough into a piping bag with a star tip. Pipe churro shapes onto parchment paper. **5.** Place the churros in the air fryer and cook for 10-12 minutes, shaking the basket halfway through. **6.** Remove the churros and dust with erythritol and cinnamon.

NUTRITIONAL INFORMATION

220 calories, 8g protein, 6g carbohydrates, 19g fat, 4g fiber, 115mg cholesterol, 70mg sodium, 85mg potassium.

Strawberry Cheesecake Bites

INGREDIENTS:

- 1 cup cream cheese, softened
- 1/4 cup powdered erythritol
- 1/2 tsp vanilla extract
- 1 large egg
- 1/4 cup almond flour
- 1 tbsp coconut flour
- 1/4 cup fresh strawberries, chopped
- 1 tbsp butter, melted
- 1 tsp lemon juice

Prep Time: 10 min   **Cook Time:10 min**   **Serves: 6**

DIRECTIONS:

1. In a bowl, mix cream cheese, erythritol, vanilla extract, and egg until smooth. **2.** Add almond flour, coconut flour, and lemon juice, stirring well. Fold in chopped strawberries. **3.** Preheat the air fryer to 320°F (160°C). **4.** Grease silicone muffin cups with melted butter and fill each with the cheesecake mixture. **5.** Place cups in the air fryer basket, ensuring they don't touch. Air fry for 8-10 minutes until the tops are set and lightly golden. **6.** Let cool in the air fryer for 5 minutes before transferring to the fridge for 30 minutes to fully set.

NUTRITIONAL INFORMATION

170 calories, 4g protein, 4g carbohydrates, 15g fat, 2g fiber, 65mg cholesterol, 100mg sodium, 90mg potassium.

Vanilla Keto Ice Cream

INGREDIENTS:

- 1 cup heavy cream
- 1/2 cup unsweetened almond milk
- 2 tbsp powdered erythritol (or keto sweetener of choice)
- 1 tsp vanilla extract
- 2 large egg yolks
- 1/4 tsp xanthan gum (optional, for thickening)

Prep Time: 10 min   **Cook Time: 8 min**   **Serves: 4**

DIRECTIONS:

1. In a saucepan, combine heavy cream and almond milk. Heat on medium until warm, but not boiling. **2.** In a separate bowl, whisk egg yolks and erythritol until smooth. **3.** Slowly pour a bit of the warm cream mixture into the egg yolk mixture while whisking continuously to temper the eggs. **4.** Return the mixture to the saucepan, stirring constantly for 3-4 minutes until it thickens slightly. **5.** Stir in vanilla extract and xanthan gum (optional). Let it cool. **6.** Transfer the mixture to a freezer-safe dish. Preheat the air fryer to 350°F (180°C). **7.** Place the dish into the air fryer for 5-8 minutes to freeze quickly, stirring occasionally.

NUTRITIONAL INFORMATION

220 calories, 2g protein, 3g carbohydrates, 21g fat, 0g fiber, 120mg cholesterol, 40mg sodium, 75mg potassium.

Keto Cinnamon Rolls

INGREDIENTS:

- 1 1/2 cups shredded mozzarella cheese
- 2 oz cream cheese
- 1 cup almond flour
- 1 tsp baking powder
- 1 large egg
- 2 tbsp butter, melted
- 2 tbsp powdered erythritol
- 1 tbsp cinnamon
- **For the Glaze:**
- 2 tbsp cream cheese
- 2 tbsp heavy cream
- 1 tbsp powdered erythritol

Prep Time: 15 min   **Cook Time:8 min**   **Serves: 4**

DIRECTIONS:

1. In a microwave-safe bowl, melt mozzarella and cream cheese for 1 minute. Stir until smooth. **2.** Mix almond flour, baking powder, and egg into the melted cheese to form dough. **3.** Roll out the dough between two sheets of parchment paper. **4.** Brush melted butter over the dough, then sprinkle with erythritol and cinnamon. **5.** Roll the dough into a log and cut into 6-8 rolls. **6.** Preheat air fryer to 350°F (180°C). Place the rolls in the basket, spaced apart. **7.** Air fry for 8 minutes, flipping halfway through.

NUTRITIONAL INFORMATION

250 calories, 10g protein, 4g carbohydrates, 22g fat, 2g fiber, 80mg cholesterol, 220mg sodium, 50mg potassium.

Keto Pecan Pie Bars

INGREDIENTS:

- **Crust:** 1 cup almond flour, 2 tbsp coconut flour, 1/4 cup melted butter, 2 tbsp erythritol.
- **Filling:** 1/2 cup chopped pecans, 1/4 cup melted butter, 1/4 cup sugar-free maple syrup, 2 tbsp erythritol, 1 large egg, 1/2 tsp vanilla extract.

Prep Time: 10 min   **Cook Time: 15 min**   **Serves: 8**

DIRECTIONS:

1. Preheat the air fryer to 325°F (160°C). **2.** Mix crust ingredients; press into a lined air fryer dish. Cook for 5 minutes. **3.** Whisk filling ingredients; pour over pre-baked crust. **4.** Top with pecans and cook at 325°F (160°C) for 8-10 minutes.

Serving Suggestion: Cool before slicing into bars.

NUTRITIONAL INFORMATION

200 calories, 3g protein, 4g carbohydrates, 19g fat, 3g fiber, 35mg cholesterol, 60mg sodium, 70mg potassium.

Low-Carb Chocolate Mousse

INGREDIENTS:

- 1 cup heavy whipping cream
- 2 tbsp unsweetened cocoa powder
- 3 tbsp powdered erythritol
- 1/2 tsp vanilla extract
- Optional: 1/4 tsp instant coffee powder for enhanced flavor

Prep Time: 5 min   **Cook Time:30 min**   **Serves: 4**

DIRECTIONS:

1. In a large bowl, whisk heavy cream, cocoa powder, erythritol, vanilla, and optional coffee powder until stiff peaks form. **2.** Spoon into serving dishes and refrigerate for 30 minutes before serving.

Serving Suggestion: Top with sugar-free whipped cream or dark chocolate shavings.

NUTRITIONAL INFORMATION

220 calories, 2g protein, 3g carbohydrates, 23g fat, 2g fiber, 80mg cholesterol, 20mg sodium, 50mg potassium.

Chapter 9: Keto Meal Plans and Bonus Materials

28-Day Keto Air Fryer Meal Plan

Week 1 Meal Plan

Breakfast:

- Day 1: Bacon-Wrapped Eggs
- Day 2: Keto Pancakes with Almond Flour
- Day 3: Cheesy Egg Bites
- Day 4: Sausage and Cheese Omelet
- Day 5: Avocado and Bacon Egg Cups
- Day 6: Spinach and Feta Breakfast Frittata
- Day 7: Zucchini and Egg Breakfast Casserole

Lunch:

- Day 1: Lemon Garlic Chicken Thighs
- Day 2: Herb-Crusted Turkey Breast
- Day 3: Chicken and Cheese Stuffed Bell Peppers
- Day 4: Air-Fried Duck Confit
- Day 5: Spicy Chicken Satay
- Day 6: Keto BBQ Ribs
- Day 7: Italian-Style Meatballs

Dinner:

- Day 1: Garlic Butter Steak Bites
- Day 2: Parmesan-Crusted Cod
- Day 3: Keto Beef Stir-Fry
- Day 4: Air-Fried Brisket with Garlic Butter
- Day 5: Garlic Butter Shrimp
- Day 6: Balsamic-Glazed Pork Loin
- Day 7: Cajun-Spiced Catfish

Snacks/Desserts:

- Day 1: Parmesan Zucchini Chips
- Day 2: Chicken Nuggets with Almond Crust
- Day 3: Coconut Macaroons
- Day 4: Air-Fried Cheese Sticks
- Day 5: Keto Chocolate Chip Cookies
- Day 6: Cheesy Stuffed Mushrooms
- Day 7: Fried Pickles with Ranch Dip

Week 2 Meal Plan

Breakfast:

- Day 1: Keto Chaffles (Cheese Waffles)
- Day 2: Keto Breakfast Burrito
- Day 3: Coconut Flour Waffles
- Day 4: Ham and Cheese Egg Rolls
- Day 5: Mushroom and Bacon Breakfast Bake
- Day 6: Keto Scotch Eggs
- Day 7: Cauliflower Hash Browns

Lunch:

- Day 1: Bacon-Wrapped Chicken Breast
- Day 2: Lemon Pepper Chicken Wings
- Day 3: Air-Fried Chicken Fajitas
- Day 4: Air-Fried Turkey Meatballs
- Day 5: Pork Belly Bites with Garlic Sauce
- Day 6: Crispy Chicken Parmesan
- Day 7: Balsamic-Glazed Pork Loin

Dinner:

- Day 1: Air-Fried Chicken Cordon Bleu
- Day 2: Keto Beef Stir-Fry

- Day 3: Herb-Crusted Lamb Chops
- Day 4: Cajun-Spiced Catfish
- Day 5: Keto Crab Cakes
- Day 6: Air-Fried Fish Tacos with Avocado Crema
- Day 7: Spicy Korean BBQ Beef

Snacks/Desserts:

- Day 1: Avocado Fries
- Day 2: Keto Deviled Eggs
- Day 3: Peanut Butter Cookies
- Day 4: Crispy Kale Chips
- Day 5: Air-Fried Cinnamon Donuts
- Day 6: Keto Cheesecake Bites
- Day 7: Parmesan-Crusted Zucchini Chips

Week 3 Meal Plan

Breakfast:

- Day 1: Keto Pancakes with Almond Flour
- Day 2: Bacon and Egg Muffins
- Day 3: Zucchini and Egg Breakfast Casserole
- Day 4: Ham and Cheese Egg Rolls
- Day 5: Coconut Flour Waffles
- Day 6: Spinach and Feta Breakfast Frittata
- Day 7: Avocado and Bacon Egg Cups

Lunch:

- Day 1: Herb-Crusted Turkey Breast
- Day 2: Air-Fried Chicken Fajitas
- Day 3: BBQ Pulled Pork
- Day 4: Lemon Garlic Chicken Thighs
- Day 5: Chicken Nuggets with Almond Crust
- Day 6: Moroccan Lamb Ribs
- Day 7: Spicy Chicken Satay

Dinner:

- Day 1: Garlic Butter Shrimp
- Day 2: Coconut Shrimp with Spicy Mayo
- Day 3: Air-Fried Brisket with Garlic Butter
- Day 4: Crispy Tuna Cakes
- Day 5: Lemon Pepper Salmon
- Day 6: Balsamic-Glazed Pork Loin
- Day 7: Garlic Butter Lobster Tails

Snacks/Desserts:

- Day 1: Air-Fried Cheese Sticks
- Day 2: Air-Fried Keto Tortillas
- Day 3: Coconut Macaroons
- Day 4: Parmesan Zucchini Chips
- Day 5: Keto Apple Fritters
- Day 6: Almond Flour Brownies
- Day 7: Air-Fried Churros

Week 4 Meal Plan

Breakfast:

- Day 1: Keto Chaffles (Cheese Waffles)
- Day 2: Cauliflower Hash Browns
- Day 3: Bacon-Wrapped Eggs
- Day 4: Cheesy Egg Bites
- Day 5: Avocado and Bacon Egg Cups
- Day 6: Mushroom and Bacon Breakfast Bake
- Day 7: Coconut Flour Waffles

Lunch:

- Day 1: Keto BBQ Ribs
- Day 2: Herb-Crusted Lamb Chops

- Day 3: Pork Belly Bites with Garlic Sauce
- Day 4: Lemon Pepper Chicken Wings
- Day 5: Air-Fried Duck Confit
- Day 6: Cajun-Spiced Chicken Wings
- Day 7: Air-Fried Chicken Cordon Bleu

Dinner:

- Day 1: Parmesan-Crusted Cod
- Day 2: Air-Fried Fish Tacos with Avocado Crema
- Day 3: Keto Salmon with Lemon and Dill
- Day 4: Balsamic-Glazed Pork Loin
- Day 5: Garlic Butter Shrimp
- Day 6: Spicy Chicken Satay
- Day 7: Keto Crab Cakes

Snacks/Desserts:

- Day 1: Air-Fried Cheese Sticks
- Day 2: Parmesan Zucchini Chips
- Day 3: Keto Chocolate Chip Cookies
- Day 4: Coconut Macaroons
- Day 5: Peanut Butter Cookies
- Day 6: Air-Fried Keto Apple Fritters
- Day 7: Keto Pumpkin Pie

Keto Grocery Shopping List

Let's be honest: success on the keto diet starts not in the kitchen, but at the grocery store. Preparation is key! If you've got all the right stuff at home, you're way less likely to give in to cravings or eat something off-plan. So, here's a grocery list to help you tackle keto cooking like a pro.

Healthy Fats and Oils

Fats are the star of the show on the keto diet, and you want them to be not just healthy, but also delicious. Here's what you should definitely throw in your cart:

- **Olive oil:** Perfect for salads and light sautéing.
- **Coconut oil:** Brings a hint of tropical flavor to your dishes and works great in baking.
- **Avocado oil:** It can handle high heat, so it's perfect for your air fryer adventures.
- **Ghee or clarified butter:** A superstar for frying without smoking up the kitchen.

Protein Sources

Keto isn't just about fats; you've got to get your protein too. Choose quality sources to keep your meals both tasty and satisfying:

- **Meat and poultry:** Chicken, beef, pork—anything you can grill or fry up. Aim for grass-fed if you can swing it.
- **Seafood:** Salmon, tuna, shrimp—all these are keto-friendly and packed with flavor!
- **Eggs:** They're a lifesaver on keto—quick to cook, great for breakfast, and perfect for snacks.

Low-Carb Vegetables

Veggies add variety to your meals, but remember the golden rule: the fewer carbs, the better! Here's what you should pick up:

- **Leafy greens:** Spinach, arugula, mixed salad greens—great for salads and side dishes.
- **Cruciferous veggies:** Cauliflower, broccoli, Brussels sprouts. Try them in the air fryer—they turn out amazing!
- **Avocados:** Not only are they low in carbs, but they're also packed with healthy fats. A true keto essential!

Nuts, Seeds, and Other Delicious Additions

Nuts and seeds are perfect for snacks and adding some crunch to your meals. Here's what should always be in your pantry:

- **Almonds and macadamia nuts:** Loaded with healthy fats and great for on-the-go munching.
- **Chia seeds and flaxseed:** Toss them into smoothies or desserts for a boost of texture and nutrition.
- **Nut butters:** Almond butter or macadamia nut butter—perfect for adding healthy fats to your dishes without the carbs.

Keto-Friendly Flours for Baking

If you can't live without baked goods, don't worry! We've got keto-friendly flour options that'll make your breads and muffins total keto winners:

- **Almond flour:** The go-to base for most keto baking—light and fluffy.
- **Coconut flour:** Adds a nice flavor to your baked goods and desserts.
- **Psyllium husk:** Helps make your bread and buns more structured and chewy.

Dairy and Cheese

If you love creamy textures and cheesy goodness in your meals, the keto diet is a dream come true! Here's what you should always have in your fridge:

- **Cheese:** Cheddar, mozzarella, parmesan—you name it, just make sure it's full-fat.
- **Creams:** Heavy cream and cream cheese are perfect for sauces, coffee, and desserts.
- **Greek yogurt:** As long as it's plain and unsweetened, it's a delicious, high-protein option.

Quick Tips for Successful Keto Grocery Shopping

1. **Stick to the outer aisles:** That's where you'll find the fresh produce, meats, and dairy products. Real food lives on the edges!
2. **Always check labels:** Watch out for hidden carbs and sugars that could sneak into your diet.
3. **Buy in bulk:** When it comes to oils, nuts, and seeds, stocking up will save you time and money!

With this shopping list, you'll always be ready to whip up some amazing keto dishes in your kitchen. And remember, preparation is everything! If you've got all the right ingredients, nothing can throw you off your keto game. Happy shopping and even happier cooking!

Measurement Conversion Chart

Hey there, keto cook! We know that sticking to a low-carb lifestyle can feel like a science sometimes, especially when it comes to getting those measurements just right. But don't worry—we've got your back! This measurement conversion chart is here to make your life in the kitchen a whole lot easier. Whether you're trying to figure out how many grams are in a cup or how to convert temperatures for your air fryer, this guide is your new best friend.

Accurate measurements are key on the keto diet because even a little too much of one ingredient can throw off your macros and potentially kick you out of ketosis. So, let's dive into the numbers and make sure you've got all the right tools to keep your keto game strong!

Basic Measurement Conversions

Dry Ingredients:

- **1 cup** = 16 tablespoons = 48 teaspoons
- **1 tablespoon** = 3 teaspoons
- **1 cup** = 8 ounces = 227 grams
- **1 ounce** = 28 grams

Liquid Ingredients:

- **1 cup** = 8 fluid ounces = 237 milliliters
- **1 tablespoon** = 15 milliliters
- **1 teaspoon** = 5 milliliters

Weight Conversions:

- **1 ounce** = 28 grams
- **1 pound** = 16 ounces = 454 grams
- **1 kilogram** = 2.2 pounds

Common Keto Ingredients

Here are some specific conversions for common keto-friendly ingredients because their texture and density can sometimes vary:

Almond Flour:

- **1 cup of almond flour** = approximately 96 grams
- **1/4 cup of almond flour** = 24 grams

Coconut Flour:

- **1 cup of coconut flour** = approximately 112 grams
- **1/4 cup of coconut flour** = 28 grams

Butter:

- **1 stick of butter = 1/2 cup** = 4 ounces = 113 grams
- **1 tablespoon of butter** = 14 grams

Cheese (shredded):

- **1 cup of shredded cheese** = approximately 113 grams
- **1/4 cup of shredded cheese** = 28 grams

Temperature Conversions

Getting your air fryer temperatures right is super important for that perfect crisp! Here's a handy guide to convert between Fahrenheit and Celsius, including some extra common air fryer settings:

- **250°F** = 120°C
- **300°F** = 150°C
- **320°F** = 160°C
- **350°F** = 175°C
- **360°F** = 180°C
- **370°F** = 188°C
- **380°F** = 193°C

- **390°F** = 200°C
- **400°F** = 200°C

Handy Tips for Measurement Conversions

1. **Invest in a digital kitchen scale:** Trust us, it's a game-changer. For the most accurate measurements, especially when baking or using low-carb flours, a digital scale ensures your macros are always on point.
2. **Spoon and level method for dry ingredients:** When you're measuring flours like almond or coconut flour, spoon them into the measuring cup and level it off with a knife. This helps avoid packing too much flour into the cup.
3. **Liquid measuring cups for liquids only:** Always use a clear liquid measuring cup with a spout for oils, water, or other liquids to get precise measurements. It really makes a difference!

Air Fryer Cooking Tips & Tricks

So, you've got your air fryer all set up, and you're ready to start cooking up some keto magic. But before you dive in, here are some tips and tricks to make sure you're getting the most out of this amazing kitchen gadget. Trust me, once you get the hang of these, you'll be air-frying like a pro in no time!

1. Don't Overcrowd the Basket

This is probably the number one rule for using your air fryer: give your food some space! The air fryer works by circulating hot air around your food, so if you pack it too full, things won't cook evenly. Lay your items out in a single layer for that perfect crispiness. If you've got a lot to cook, just do it in batches—it's totally worth the extra few minutes.

2. Preheat Your Air Fryer

Yep, just like your oven, preheating your air fryer makes a big difference. It helps the food cook evenly and gives you that delicious golden-brown finish. Most air fryers heat up pretty quickly, so just give it a few minutes to get nice and hot before adding your ingredients.

3. Lightly Coat with Oil (When Needed)

One of the best things about the air fryer is that you can use way less oil than traditional frying. But sometimes a little spritz of oil can go a long way to make your food even crispier. Use a spray bottle or a brush to lightly coat your ingredients, and you'll be amazed at the results!

4. Shake Things Up

If you're cooking smaller items like fries or veggie chips, give the basket a good shake halfway through the cooking process. This helps to ensure that everything cooks evenly and all sides get that perfect crunch. Plus, it's a great excuse to check on your tasty snacks!

5. Keep It Clean

I know, I know—cleaning isn't the most fun part of cooking. But keeping your air fryer clean is super important to make sure it works its best. After each use, make sure to wipe out any crumbs or grease. And don't worry, most baskets are dishwasher safe, which makes cleanup a breeze!

6. Adjust Cooking Times and Temperatures

Air fryers can be a little different from your traditional oven, so don't be afraid to tweak the cooking times and temperatures. Start with lower times and check your food often. It's always easier to cook it a little longer than to rescue it from being overdone!

7. Experiment with Different Foods

The air fryer isn't just for fries and chicken wings! Try using it to roast veggies, bake low-carb keto bread, or even make crispy bacon. The sky's the limit, so don't be afraid to get creative and try out new recipes. You might just discover your next favorite dish!

With these tips and tricks in your back pocket, you'll be air-frying up a storm in no time. The air fryer is a total game-changer, especially for us keto lovers, so go ahead and make the most of it. Happy cooking, and may all your meals be crispy and delicious!

Made in the USA
Monee, IL
06 January 2025